ACT! for Windows

Shelley O'Hara

ACT! for Windows

Shelley O'Hara

SAMS
PUBLISHING

Sams Publishing

A Division of Macmillan Computer Publishing
201 West 103rd Street
Indianapolis, Indiana 46290

ISBN: 1-56686-143-8

Library of Congress Catalog No.: 93-75011

Printing Code: The rightmost double-digit number is the year of the book's printing; the rightmost single-digit number is the number of the book's printing. For example, 94-1 shows that the first printing of the book occurred in 1994.

97 96 95   5

Manufactured in the United States of America

About the Author

Shelley O'Hara has recently started her own technical writing and training company in Indianapolis. She has written over 25 computer books, including the best-selling *Easy Windows*, *Easy DOS*, *Easy 1-2-3*, and *Easy WordPerfect*. O'Hara has a bachelor of arts in English from the University of South Carolina and a master of arts in English from the University of Maryland.

Credits

Acknowledgments

Special thanks to the following individuals for their role in creating this book:

Rick Ranucci, Publisher of Brady, for giving me the opportunity to write this book and for providing suggestions on how to make the book better.

Gordon E. Eubanks, Jr., Symantec CEO, for writing the foreword to this book.

Greg Head, ACT! Product Manager, for his insights into ACT! and the users of ACT!.

Steve Haigh, Special Sales Representative for Prentice Hall Computer Publishing, for giving me his views as a super salesman using ACT!.

Don Eamon, Developmental Editor, for asking the right questions.

Howard Jones, Production Editor, for the careful editing job.

Bill Fletcher, Software Showcase Consultants, and Art Karp, PC Works, both dedicated ACT! users, for taking the time to discuss their views of the product and their views of the ideal book on the product.

Robert Waring and Bill Beikman, Technical Editors, for ensuring the accuracy of the text.

Contents at a Glance

Contents

Foreword

ACT!'s great success is due in large part to the support of the community of ACT! enthusiasts who have improved the product through their technical contributions, suggestions, and value added solutions. ACT! 2.0 has benefited significantly from this dedicated group of customers.

With this new version of ACT! we are addressing the needs of a growing number of ACT! users both in large organizations and small businesses. *Brady's official guide to ACT! for Windows* is the perfect companion to ACT! 2.0. It offers easy-to-follow instructions and real world tips to help you get the most from ACT!. Whether you're a new or advanced user, this book will help you use ACT! more proficiently and tailor the software to meet your needs.

Gordon E. Eubanks, Jr.

President and CEO Symantec

Introduction

"ACT! is like a money machine."

"ACT! allows me to relax. I don't worry about forgetting to make an important call."

"In the morning, I turn on the computer and ACT! has my schedule all ready. I know just what I need to do on that day."

"ACT! gives me the tools to make the sale."

These remarks are from dedicated ACT! users. They know and appreciate the many benefits of using ACT! contact manager. With ACT! and this book, you too can better manage your schedule and contacts so that you have time to concentrate on what's important—your business.

What Makes ACT! So Powerful

ACT! does more than track names, addresses, and phone numbers. It provides a large number of tools to help you manage and communicate with your contacts. ACT! helps you in the following four ways:

1. ACT! provides a way to keep track of key information about your contacts—customers, clients, suppliers, reps, and so on.

2. ACT! enables you to schedule calls, meetings, and to-do items so that you know what you need to accomplish and when.

3. ACT! makes it easy to prepare written communications—reports, letters, memos, and more.

4. ACT! includes features that make maintaining your data easy.

Contact Database

The main tool or document in ACT! is the contact database. The following list summarizes the key database features:

✔ You can use the predefined database or customize the database to suit your needs.

✔ You can create and use more than one database.

✔ You can view the database in different layouts—for instance, view a contact list.

✔ You can enter, sort, and find any records in the database.

Setting up and entering data is covered in Part I of this book.

Scheduling

Keeping track of the calls, meetings, and activities in your day can be a headache. But these activities are vital to your success. If you promised a client that you would call on a certain day and forget to do so, your business may suffer. If you schedule a meeting with your sales representatives and then are late to that meeting, what kind of image do you project? ACT! provides several features to make it easy to track calls, meetings, and activities. The following list highlights the key scheduling features:

✔ You can schedule calls, meetings, or to-do items.

✔ You can tell ACT! to alert you when you have a call or meeting.

✔ You can have ACT! make the calls for you. If necessary, you can use the timer to time the call.

✔ You can view a calendar of scheduled activities.

Scheduling is covered in Part II of this book.

Documents

Phone calls may not be the only means of communication with your clients. You may need to send a letter or fax. If you manage a team of sales people, you may need to send a memo to your sales staff. ACT! enables you to create the following documents:

✔ You can use a predesigned format to quickly create a memo, letter, or fax cover sheet. You can easily insert information from your contact database into the memo, letter, or fax.

✔ You can create a form letter to send to many clients or customers. You can also create mailing labels.

✔ If the predesigned templates don't suit your needs, you can use the word processing program to create and format any type of document you need.

✔ You can create reports of scheduled activities, client lists, and more.

Documents are covered in Part III of this book.

Customizing and Maintaining ACT!

If the program isn't set up in just the way you work, you can customize it to suit your needs. You also need a way to maintain—back up, purge, compress—the database. Customization and maintenance are the focus of Part IV.

What Makes This Book Special

This book is designed so that finding key information is easy. Short, focused chapters make it easy to turn to the topic of interest. Numbered steps and figures illustrate all key procedures so that you can follow along without trouble.

This book highlights time management tips and program tips so that you can learn how to make the best use of both your time and the program.

Words or commands that you are asked to type on the keyboard are shown in a **bold** typeface.

This book is designed with the same purpose as the ACT! program—to make you better at your job.

PART

I

Contacts

Sales Scenario

The rewards of using ACT! in a sales job can be enormous. Imagine this scenario:

When you come into the office in the morning, you turn on your computer, start ACT!, and review your daily calendar. This daily calendar includes all the calls, meetings, and to-do items you need to complete for the day. You know exactly what you need to accomplish on this day.

You start with phone calls. Using the calendar, you quickly display the first contact you need to call. You review the contact information, which you can customize so that it contains just the information you need. You can track, for instance, the last results and the next objective. You review notes about your conversations with this contact and are prepared with all the key information you need to make an effective call.

Using ACT!, you display the pertinent phone numbers for this contact and have ACT! dial the number. You pick up the phone and talk with the contact. The contact is impressed with how prepared you are and how much you remember from the last conversation. You make a sale.

You follow up the order with a letter of confirmation and thanks, created quickly and almost automatically with ACT!

Next, you record the results of the call so that you are just as prepared for future calls. ACT! puts away the contact screen and displays the next contact you need to call.

You are on to your next call—and your next sale.

You can do all this and more with ACT!. The book gives you details on how to put all ACT! features to work. This scenario gives you some tips on using ACT! in a sales environment.

Contact Screen

The key to making an effective sales call is staying informed. You should use the contact screen to track key data about your contact. Some information is a given—name, address, phone numbers, assistants, and so on. ACT! also provides "extra" fields that you can define and use how you want. The first thing you should do to set up ACT! for maximum benefit is to customize the contact screens.

The screen shown in figure S.1.1 was customized for a greeting card and calendar salesperson. This salesperson tracks the size of the stores, items sold, and other key information.

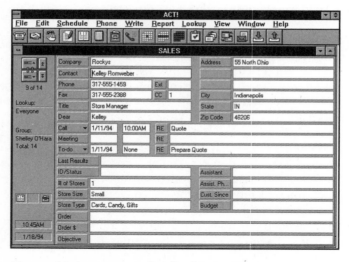

Figure S1.1. A customized sales contact screen.

The second tool that may be useful is the reference library. You can use this feature to store a script or a price list. This salesperson uses the reference library to store a price list so that the prices are always available (see fig. S1.2).

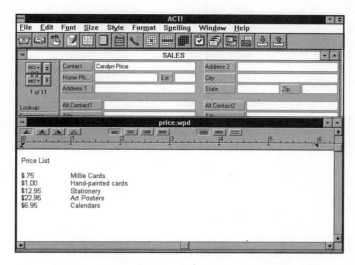

Figure S1.2. A price list used as the reference library.

You can customize the user fields and reference library, as described in Chapter 3, "Managing Contacts."

Reports

Rather than track numbers and names using an address book or Rolodex, use ACT! to store the information. You can print out Rolodex cards or a phone list so that your information is always up-to-date. Figure S1.3 shows an address list.

If you travel, you can print out your weekly or daily calendar to take with you. Figure S1.4 shows a weekly calendar.

```
Darlene Ball
   President                            Phone: 317-255-9731
   Darlene's Gagdets                    Fax: 317-555-1209
   IN 46220
```

```
Ann Bondi
   Store Manager                        Phone: 217-555-8711
   Surprise!                            Home Phone: 217-555-0666
   560 Chatty Street                    Fax: 217-555-9111
   Champaign, IL 61832

   55 Mary Street Champaign, IL 61832
```

```
Barb Cage
   Sales Manager                        Phone: 207-555-9011
   The Perfect Gift                     Home Phone: 207-555-48884
   1200 Iron Street                     Fax: 207-555-4788
   Williamsburg, VA 23185

   809 Plum Williamsburg, VA 23185
```

```
Maureen Cates
   Purchasing Manager                   Phone: 803-555-6711
   Carolina Cards                       Home Phone: 803-555-8911
   6708 Little O Street                 Fax: 803-555-6188
   Columbia, SC 29212

   709 Green Street Columbia, SC 29227

   Alt Contact1: Bob Daugherty  803-555-1991
```

```
Carole Gill
   Regional Manager                     Phone: 502-555-9011
   Fun City                             Home Phone: 502-555-4311
   6709 Derby Lane                      Fax: 502-555-6099
   Louisville, KY 40207

   7809 South River Street Lousiville, KY 40207

   Alt Contact1: Patrick Yates  502-555-5011

   Referred by: Kathleen Marbaugh
```

Figure S1.3. An address list.

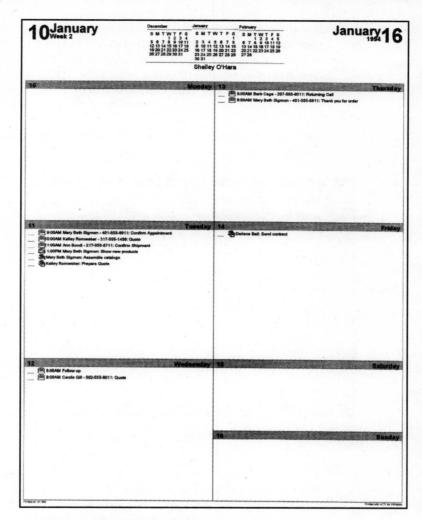

Figure S1.4. A weekly calendar.

Correspondence

ACT! provides predefined letters, memos, and fax cover sheets that you can use to quickly create these types of documents. You should also consider the following two ideas:

✔ If you create the same type of document over and over, consider creating a template. For instance, you may have a letter that you use to confirm a sale and thank a customer. Rather than create the letter over and over, set up a template so that the letter is always available, and type in the client's name and address to create personalized letters. You can even add the template to the menu.

Chapter 11 discusses templates. ACT! provides a sales order form that you might want to use (see fig. S1.5).

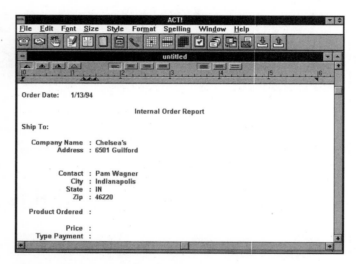

Figure S1.5. An order form.

✔ If you need to send the same letter to several people, you can create a form letter. ACT! merges the names and addresses from the contact screen with the letter you type to create personalized letters for each contact. Form letters also are covered in Chapter 11.

Special Sales

ACT! has set up the contact database for some special sales positions. To use these databases, you apply a database description file, as described in Chapter 12, "Customizing ACT!."

If you are in insurance sales, take a look at the INSURANC description file, shown in figure S1.6.

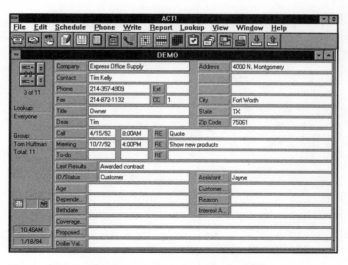

Figure S1.6. The insurance description file.

If you are in commercial real estate, the COMMRE file may work as a starting point for your own customized database (see fig. S1.7).

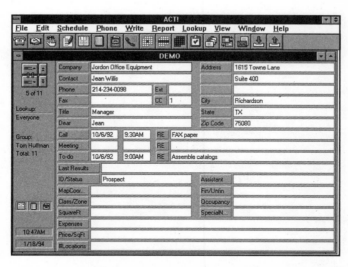

Figure S1.7. The commercial real estate description file.

Residential real estate agents should investigate the RESRE set up (see fig. S1.8).

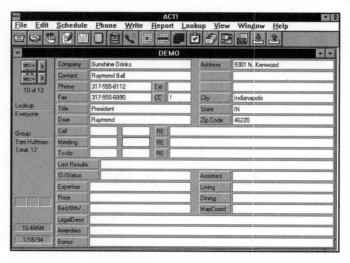

Figure S1.8. The residential real estate description file.

Sales managers might start from the MANAGER file and then make changes to the database, as needed. Figure S1.9 shows this description file.

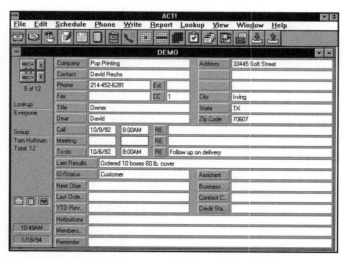

Figure S1.9. The manager description file.

Getting Started

ACT! for Windows is a contact management program designed to make keeping track of contacts, meetings, calls, and activities simple and easy. The names, addresses, and phone numbers of your clients or associates are vital to your business. This program can help you manage this critical information so that you can concentrate on your business. With ACT! you don't need to assemble and track scraps of paper with information. You can enter the information on-screen and quickly and easily retrieve the information.

This chapter covers the following topics:

- Starting ACT!

- Understanding the database screen

- Using the icon bar

- Getting help

- Exiting ACT!

Starting ACT!

Before you can start ACT!, you first must start Windows. On some computers, Windows starts automatically when you turn on the computer. On other computers, you see a DOS prompt (such as C:\>) when you turn on the computer. In this case, you must give the command to start Windows. Follow these steps:

1. Type WIN.

2. Press Enter.

The Program Manager appears on-screen (see fig. 1.1). For more information about Windows and the Program Manager, consult your Windows manual.

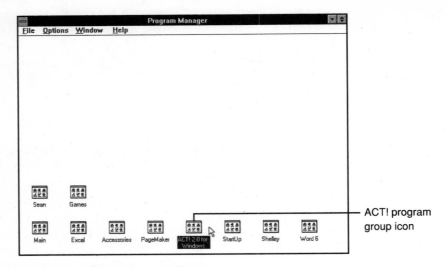

ACT! program
group icon

Figure 1.1. The Program Manager.

You start ACT! just as you start any other Windows program. Follow these steps:

1. Double-click the ACT! program group icon.

   The ACT! program group icon is probably named ACT! 2.0 for Windows. Double-clicking on the icon opens the group window. You see the program icon (see fig. 1.2).

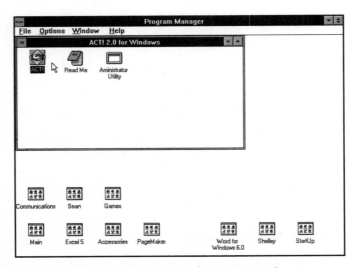

Figure 1.2. The ACT! program group window.

2. Double-click the ACT! program icon.

   The program starts.

Depending on when you start the program, you may see the following screens:

✔ If you are starting the program for the first time, you may see a background and the File and Help menus, or ACT! may open and display the DEMO database. You can choose to open a database or create a new database. You can use this database to practice moving around.

✔ If you have already created a database, you see that database on-screen.

TIP: *If you want ACT! to start each time you start Windows, drag the program icon to the Startup group in Windows.*

What Is Windows?

Windows is a graphical user interface (GUI, pronounced gooey). That means that the environment uses pictures and other on-screen elements to make it easy to start programs, select commands, and perform other tasks. If you've ever used DOS (the command line interface), you'll quickly realize the benefits of using Windows.

In short, Windows offers these benefits:

✔ *Starting programs is as simple as pointing to the program icon and double-clicking the mouse button.*

✔ *Most Windows programs operate in a similar manner. Once you learn one program, you can quickly pick up the basics of others.*

✔ *You can start more than one program and copy information back and forth between programs.*

✔ *Windows provides many additional tools, including a file manager, a control panel for customizing Windows, a calculator, and many others.*

Understanding the Screen

ACT! puts many tools on-screen for quick access. Figure 1.3 identifies the key parts of the database screen.

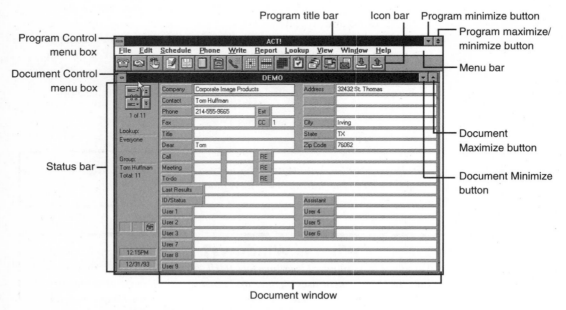

Figure 1.3. The ACT! database screen.

The following checklist shows key screen elements:

✔ In Windows, the actual program is contained in one window. Within the program window, you see the document window. Each window has its own set of controls and can be moved and resized.

✔ Double-click the program Control menu box to close the program. Click the Restore button to shrink the size of the window so that it doesn't fill the entire screen. Click the Minimize button to reduce the program window to an icon.

✔ Double-click the document Control menu box to close the document window, but keep the program running. Click the document Maximize button to enlarge the document window so that it fills the entire screen. Click the document Minimize button to reduce the document window to an icon.

✔ The menu bar lists the names of the menus. To select a menu command, click on the menu name. Then click on the command you want. Some commands display submenus; click on the command you want in the submenu. Some commands display dialog boxes. Make the selections you want and choose OK.

✔ The icon bar provides quick access to frequently used commands or features. See the section "Using the Icon Bar" for information on the icon bar.

✔ The status bar provides information about the current record. You can use the buttons in this bar to move from record to record. See Chapter 2 for more information.

✔ To hide the status bar, choose the Window Hide Status Bar command. Choose the Window Show Status Bar to turn the status bar back on. Only one option appears at a time.

✔ If you have a database open and one or more document windows open—for example, a word processing document and a database—you can display both windows. Open the Window menu. Choose the Cascade command to show the database windows stacked on top of each other. Choose Tile to arrange all open windows in panes on-screen.

✔ To move among open windows, click on the window you want if the window is visible. Or open the Window menu. At the bottom of the window, each open window is listed. Click on the window you want.

TIP: *If you don't have a mouse or if you prefer to keep your hands on the keyboard, you can use the keyboard to select a menu command. Press the Alt key to activate the menu bar. Press the key letter (underlined) in the menu name. Press the key letter in the command name.*

Using the Icon Bar

The icon bar provides quick access to frequently used commands. To use the icon bar, you must have a mouse. Point to the icon you want and click the mouse button. Table 1.1 lists the icon bars and their functions.

> **TIP:** *Some commands have keyboard shortcuts, listed next to the command on the menu. You can press the key combination to access the command without opening the menu. For example, press Ctrl+S to select the File Save command.*

Table 1.1

Icon bar	Function
	Schedules a call
	Schedules a meeting
	Schedules a to-do activity
	Creates a letter
	Displays an activity list
	Displays notes
	Displays client history
	Displays phone list
	Displays a day view of scheduled activities
	Displays a week view of scheduled activities

Icon bar	Function
	Displays a month view of scheduled activities
	Displays a task list
	Displays a contact list
	Toggles between current and previous layouts
	Creates an e-mail message
	Opens your inbox
	Opens your outbox

TIP: *You can add icons to the bar, and you can move the icon bar to a different location on-screen. Chapter 12 covers customizing the icon bar.*

Time-Management Tip

As you work through your day, ask periodically "Is this the best use of my time right now?" If it is not the best use of time, make a change.

Getting Help

If you can't remember how to perform a feature or if you can't remember what a feature does, you can display on-line help. You can use on-line help to remind you how to accomplish a task or to find out what a command does. This section explains the help options.

Time-Management Tip

Before you start a task, organize first. Be sure that you have all the tools you need for the job. Collect and arrange the tools so that the information and tools you need are handy.

Using the Help Index

If you want to look up a particular topic or task, use the Help index. Follow these steps:

1. Click Help in the menu bar.

   You see the Help menu.

2. Click the Index command.

   You see the Help Index (see fig. 1.4).

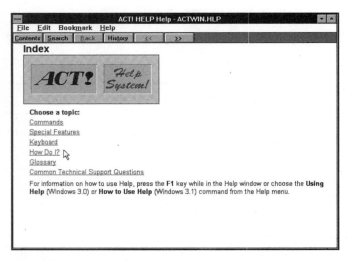

Figure 1.4. The Help Index.

TIP: *Press F1 to display the Help Contents. If you have a dialog box open on-screen and need help, press F1. Pressing F1 in this case displays help about the dialog box rather than the Help Contents.*

---

3. Click the How Do I? option.

You can click any green or underlined topic to jump to that topic. How Do I? helps you find the steps necessary to complete a task.

TIP: *To get a definition of a term, choose the Help Glossary command. Then click on the term that you want defined. ACT! displays a popup definition for the term.*

---

4. Click on the task for which you want help.

You can click on any green or underlined topic. The procedures are divided into groups, so you need to continue selecting topics until the help information is displayed. Figure 1.5 shows help information on Inserting a New Contact.

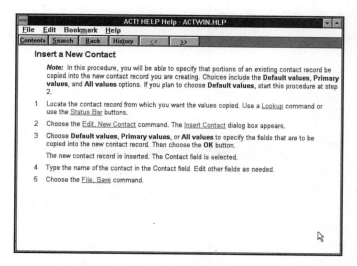

Figure 1.5. Help on inserting a new contact.

Navigating through the Help System

If you select a wrong topic and want to back up or if you want to start from the top, you can use the buttons beneath the menu bar:

Button	Description
Contents	To return to the Contents screen, click this button.
Search	To search for help, click this button. See the next section.
Back	Click this button to move to the previous help screen.
History	Click this button to display a list of topics you have looked up. To move to another topic, double-click on the new topic in the list.
<<	Click this button to move to the previous related topic in the group.
>>	Click this button to move to the next related topic in the group.

Searching for Help

If you cannot find the topic you want by navigating through the lists, you can search for help. Follow these steps:

1. Click Help in the menu bar.

   You see the Help menu.

2. Click the Index command.

   You see the Help Index.

3. Click the Search button.

   You see the Search dialog box (see fig. 1.6).

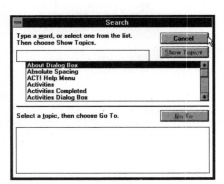

Figure 1.6. The Search dialog box.

4. Type the topic on which you want help.

   You can type all or part of the entry. As you type, ACT! will display matching topics in the list box beneath the text box.

5. In the list box, click on the topic.

   You can scroll through the list box until the topic you want appears.

6. Click the Show Topics button.

   You see a list of topics in the bottom half of the dialog box.

7. Click on the topic you want.

8. Click the Go To button.

ACT! displays help information on the selected topic.

Time-Management Tip

Organize your workspace so that it is comfortable and quiet. Make sure that you have all the tools you need.

Getting Context-Sensitive Help

You can get help about a command or a keyboard shortcut. Follow these steps:

1. Press Shift+F1.

   The mouse pointer changes to a question mark and pointer.

2. Do one of the following:

   To get help on a particular command, choose the command. You see help information on the selected command.

   To get help on a keyboard shortcut, press the key combination. ACT! displays help on the keyboard shortcut. (If no keyboard shortcut is assigned to the key combination you press, nothing happens.)

Double-click the Help window's Control menu box to close the Help window.

> **CAUTION:** *Never, if at all possible, shut off the computer while ACT! is running.*

Exiting ACT!

After you finish working in ACT!, you should save all documents and exit the program. Saving a database is covered in Chapter 2. Saving other documents is covered in Chapter 7.

Follow these steps:

1. Click File in the menu bar.

   You see the File menu.

2. Click the Exit command.

You are returned to the Windows Program Manager. You can start another Windows program or exit Windows and turn off the computer.

> **TIP:** *Press Alt+F4 to select the File Exit command.*

Q&A

I can't find the ACT! program icon or group. Where is it?

✔ When you install ACT!, the installation program creates a program group and icon (or under various desktop programs, it may be hidden in a group window of some sort). If you haven't installed the program, you need to do so. See Appendix A.

✔ You can have many windows open at once in Windows. It could be that an open window is hiding the ACT! program group icon. Close all windows and look for the icon.

✔ You can move the program icon to another program group if you want. Try opening other windows to see if someone has moved the program icon to another group.

How do I close a menu without making a selection?

✔ To close a menu without making a selection, press Esc or click outside the menu.

Setting Up a Contact Database

Your contacts are the most vital part of your business. With ACT! you can keep track not only of the names, addresses, and phone numbers of your contacts, but also of information that helps you make a sale. For example, you can track close dates, rollover dates, and other key dates. You can keep notes about your last conversations with a contact so that you know where you are in the sales process. The key to successful contact management is in setting up the contact database. In this chapter, you learn how to:

- Create a new database
- Add contacts
- Enter contact information
- Move from record to record
- Customize the database
- Save the database
- View the database

What is a Database?

A database is a collection of related information—similar to a Rolodex. The contact database tracks the same or similar information for each person or client—name, company name, address, phone number, and so on. The information about one contact is called a record. The individual pieces that make up that record are called fields. For example, you have fields for the last name, first name, company name, address, and so on.

Creating a New Database

When you first start ACT!, you may see a blank background with two menus in the menu bar, or the DEMO database.

When you create a new database, give some thought to what information you need to keep. The database has set fields for common information such as the company name, contact name, address, city, state, ZIP codes, fax number, assistant, and more. You can customize the database to include any additional fields you need. See the section, "Customizing the Contact Database," for more information.

> **TIP:** *Keep in mind that after a database is set up, it is difficult to make changes to the structure of the database. Spend some time thinking about the information you need to do business.*

Follow these steps to create a new database:

1. Choose the File New command.

   Remember, to choose a command you first click on the menu name in the menu bar. Then click on the command. You also can use the keyboard. See Chapter 1 for more information on choosing commands.

   You see the New File dialog box (see fig. 2.1). Here you select the type of file you want to create.

> **TIP:** *Press Ctrl+N to select the File New command.*

Figure 2.1. The New File dialog box.

2. Choose Database.

   You see the New Database dialog box (see fig. 2.2). Here you type the name of the database.

Figure 2.2. The New Database dialog box.

3. Type a name for the database.

   You can type up to 8 characters. ACT! uses the extension DBF by default. If you use only one database, the database name can be generic (CLIENTS, CONTACTS, and so on). If you plan to use more than one database—for example, to track different types of contacts—use a more descriptive name.

4. Choose OK.

   You see the Enter "My Record" Information dialog box (see fig. 2.3). In this dialog box, you enter information about yourself. If you completed this information when you installed the program, some or all of the fields may be complete. You can make any changes. If the entries are correct, skip to step 13.

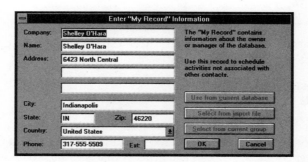

Figure 2.3. The Enter "My Record" Information dialog box.

5. Type your company name and press Tab.

   Pressing Tab moves you to the next field in the record.

6. Type your name and press Tab.

7. Type your address and press Tab. If needed, complete the other address lines. If not, press Tab until you move to City.

8. Type your city and press Tab.

9. Type your state and press Tab.

10. Type your ZIP code and press Tab.

11. Type your country and press Tab.

12. Type your phone number and press Tab. If you have an extension, type that next.

13. Choose OK.

    You are asked whether the information is correct.

14. Choose Yes if the information is correct. If you choose No, you are returned to the Enter "My Record" Information dialog box to make further changes. After making more changes, click OK, and then choose Yes.

    You are prompted for a password.

15. If you want to assign a password to the database, type it and choose OK. You'll have to retype it to verify the password and choose OK a second time. Otherwise, just choose OK.

TIP: *If you choose Cancel, the database is not created.*

Your record is now complete. ACT! displays the contact database screen. Here you can enter information about your contacts.

Adding New Contacts

When you create a new database, the first record displayed is your personal record. This record is useful for scheduling activities that don't involve other contacts. You can add other contacts easily. To enter other contacts, follow these steps:

1. Choose the Edit New Contact command.

> **TIP:** *Press Ins to choose the Edit New Contact command.*

You see the Insert Contact dialog box (see fig. 2.4).

Figure 2.4. The Insert Contact dialog box.

You can customize the database so that certain fields are completed automatically. For example, if all your contacts are in Illinois, you can have ACT! enter IL for the State field for all contacts. For information on customizing the contact screen, see "Customizing the Contact Database."

2. Choose one of the following new contact options:

Choose	To...
Default	Insert all the default values you have assigned.
Primary	Insert the same values used in the current record for all primary fields. You can assign which fields are primary fields. See the section "Customizing the Contact Database."
All	Insert all the values from the current record in the new record.

You see a record on-screen. Depending on which option you chose, some fields already may be completed.

Entering Contact Information

You can store two screens of information about each contact. The first screen, shown in figure 2.5, contains the following information:

✔ The contact's name, address, phone number, and company name.

✔ The contact's title.

✔ The contact's secretary's name.

✔ The name you use to address the contact (Dear).

✔ An area to schedule activities (Call, Meeting, or To-do) for the contact.

✔ The results from your last call or meeting (Last Results).

✔ The identification or status of the contact (ID/Status).

✔ Nine fields (User 1-9) that you can customize to suit your own purposes. See the section, "Customizing the Contact Database."

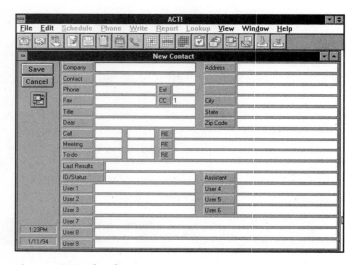

Figure 2.5. The first contact screen.

Completing the First Screen

To enter information, type the first entry and press Tab. When you enter a contact name, enter it using the same format for all contacts. You can use the format First Name Last Name. ACT! knows how to separate the two. Or you can use the format Last Name, First Name. You can also type a prefix, such as Ms. For information on adding or changing the prefixes ACT! recognizes, see Chapter 12. Press Tab to move to the next field in the database. When you first enter contact records, you probably will complete only the top part of the contact record. Information about calls, meetings, to-do items, results, and other things are entered later as you start to use the contact database.

ACT! moves through the fields in this order: Company, Contact, Phone, Ext, Fax, CC (Country Code), Title, Dear, Address, City, State, Zip Code. If you make a mistake, you can press Shift+Tab to move backwards through the fields.

Some fields contain popup menus. Rather than type a value, you can display the popup menu and then select the entry you want. To display the popup, press F2. Then click on the item you want. Choose OK. For example, in the Title field, press F2 to display a list of titles (see fig 2.6).

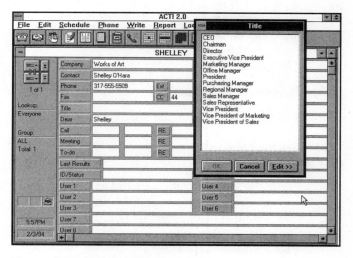

Figure 2.6. A popup menu.

TIP: *You can edit the popup menus so that they contain the entries you most commonly make in your contact database. See the section, "Customizing the Contact Database."*

The following table lists some of the fields for which popups are available:

Field	Description of Popup
Phone	Lists common area codes
Fax	Lists common area codes
Title	Lists common job titles
CC	Lists country codes
City	Lists common cities
State	Lists states and state abbreviations
Zip Code	Initially blank, but can be used to list common ZIP codes
Last Results	Lists last results—for example, Got appointment
ID/Status	Lists customer IDs—for example, Competitor, Customer, and so on

When you complete all the pertinent fields in the first record, you can move to and complete the second screen.

Completing the Second Screen

To move to the second screen, do one of the following:

✔ Click the Previous Layout icon to toggle to the second screen (First time, this shows only contact 1).

✔ Choose the View Layout command and choose the Contact 2 option.

You see the second contact screen (see fig. 2.7).

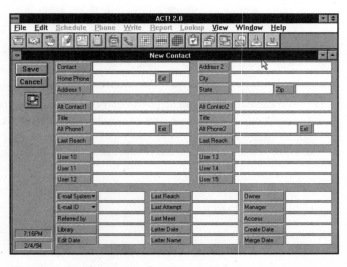

Figure 2.7. The second contact screen.

The following table describes the fields and popups available for this screen:

Field	Description	Popup
Contact	Contact Name carried over from first screen.	
Home Phone	Home or other phone number for contact.	Lists common area codes.
Ext	Extension.	
Address 1 and 2	Alternate address for contact.	
City	City for alternate address.	Lists common cities.
State	State for alternate address.	Lists states and state abbreviations.
Zip	Zip for alternate address.	
Alt Contact 1	Name(s) of alternate contact.	
Alt Contact 2	Enter the person to contact if the initial contact is not available. You can enter names, titles, and phone numbers for two additional contacts.	
Title	Title of alternate contact.	Lists common job titles.
Alt Phone 1	Phone numbers of alternate contact.	Lists common area codes.
Alt Phone 2		
Ext	Extension.	
Last Reach	Date you last spoke with this contact.	
User 10-15	User-defined fields. See "Customizing the Contact Database."	
E-mail System	Name of E-mail system used Displays E-mail address. See Chapter 6.	
E-mail ID	ID for E-mail.	
Referred by	Name of person referred.	
Library	Type the name of the reference library you want to attach to this contact. See "Customizing the Contact Database."	

continues

Field	Description	Popup
Edit Date	Date the record was last edited. ACT! will enter this date automatically. You can overwrite the date, if necessary.	
Last Reach	Date you last contacted person.	
Last Attempt	Date you last attempted to contact person.	
Last Meet	Date you last met with contact. ACT! will enter this date automatically. You can edit the date, if necessary.	
Letter Date	Date you sent last letter. ACT! will enter this date automatically. You can edit the date, if necessary.	
Letter Name	File name of the letter you sent. ACT! enters this name automatically.	
Owner	Name of the company.	
Manager	Name of the company manager.	
Access	Access level of record (Exclude or Include).	Displays two options.
Create Date	Date record was created.	
Merge Date	Date record was merged.	

To return to the first screen, press F6, click the Previous Layout icon, or choose the View Layout Contact 1 command.

Saving the Record

After you complete all the fields in the record, click the Save button to save the database and the new record. You can also choose the File Save command or press Ctrl+S to save the database and record.

If you want to cancel the entries, click the Cancel button.

Time-Saving Tip

Take some time collecting and entering all the information you have about a contact. You may invest some time at first, but this time pays off when you can find the information you need quickly and easily.

Attaching Notes to a Contact

As you enter information or work with clients, you may want to keep a note about the client. It may be helpful to note how long the person has been on the job, key opinions of the person, or other personal or professional information. If you want to attach a free-form note (not field information), you can do so.

Follow these steps to add a note:

1. Choose the View Notes command.

TIP: *Press F9 to choose the View Notes command or click the Notes* 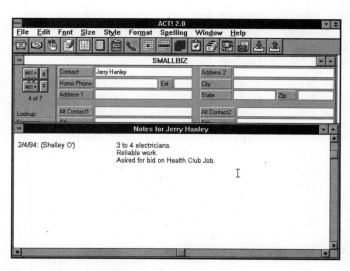 *button.*

ACT! opens a note window. The date and your first name and last initial are entered automatically.

2. Type the text for the note.

You can type as much text as needed. Figure 2.8 shows a note added to a contact.

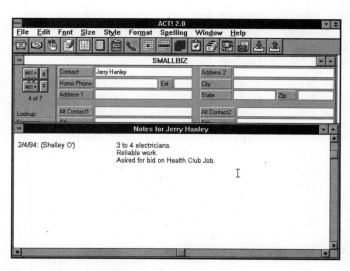

Figure 2.8. A contact note.

3. After you finish typing the note, double-click the Control menu box for the Note window to close the window.

You return to the contact screen. When a note is attached to a contact, the Note indicator appears in the status bar.

To edit or view the note, choose the View Notes command, press F9, or click the Notes button.

Adding Other Information

As you work with your contacts, other information will be added to the contact database—scheduled calls, meetings, to-do items, and more. See Chapter 4 for information on scheduling calls, meetings, and to-do items.

Calls, meetings, and to-do list items are tracked in the client history. Viewing the client history is covered in Chapter 5.

Data Entry Tips

The first few records you enter may take some time, but after you get the hang of entering records, consider the following data-entry techniques:

- ✔ If you have several contacts at the same company, display the record for one of the contacts. Choose Edit New Contact and choose Primary. ACT! creates a new record and uses the same company, phone, fax, country code, address, city, state, and zip. You can enter the contact name, title, and extension for this particular contact. You also can change which fields are tagged as primary fields. See "Customizing the Contact Database."

- ✔ If you enter the same information in all your records—for instance, the state—define a default value. See the section, "Customizing the Contact Database."

- ✔ For maximum benefit of the contact information, you should define and use the user fields. The section "Customizing the Contact Database" gives you some ideas about how these fields can be used to help your business.

- ✔ In addition to information about the contact, you can also enter and keep track of notes and client histories. These topics are covered in the next chapter.

Moving Around and Using the Status Bar

After you enter a few records in your contact database, you need to learn how to move from record to record. When there are just a few records, moving around is easy. You can quickly scan through them.

When you have many records, you need to use a different method for finding a record you want. Instead of flipping through the contacts like a Rolodex, you can have the computer search for the record you want. The following chapter discusses more record-finding techniques.

The status bar on the left side of the contact screen gives you information about the current record (see fig. 2.9). The status bar also provides buttons that enable you to move from record to record.

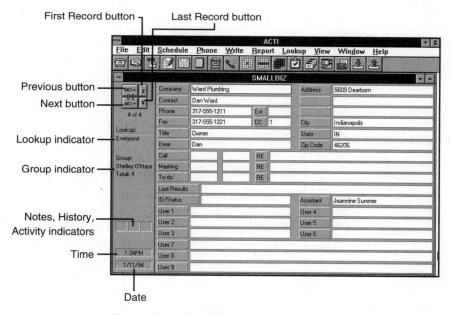

Figure 2.9. The Status Bar.

Moving from Record to Record

To move from record to record, you can do any of the following:

✔ Move to the next record by clicking the Next button or pressing Page Down.

✔ Move to the previous record by clicking the Previous button or pressing Page Up.

✔ Move to the first record by clicking the First Record button.

✔ Move to the last record by clicking the Last Record button.

Understanding Record Status

The other items in the status bar provide information about the current record. The status bar displays the following information:

✔ The current record number as well as the total number of records (2 of 10, for example).

✔ The current lookup group. The following chapter explains lookup groups.

✔ The current group indicator. The following chapter explains groups.

✔ If the contact has any notes attached, any activities scheduled, or a history, you see icons for each of these items.

✔ The current date and time.

Customizing the Contact Database

The contact database is what you make it. It can be a replacement for your Rolodex or a program that helps you sell more, track information, and manage your time. One key to successful contact management is in setting up the database so that it is as effective as possible.

You can customize the database in five key ways:

✔ To save time while entering records, you can define default values for the fields in the contact database.

✔ Another time-saving technique for data entry is modifying the popup lists so that they contain entries pertinent to your business.

✔ You can modify the field attributes for the database fields—specify which fields have popups, which fields are primary fields, and more.

✔ Setting up and using the user-defined fields can help you maximize the quantity and quality of information you track about a client.

✔ If you follow a set script or need to have a reference list handy, use the reference libraries.

This section discusses each of these customize options.

TIP: *This section discusses customizing the database. For information on customizing the program, see Chapter 12, "Customizing ACT!."*

Time-Saving Tip

Most techniques that save time require up-front work. Initially you may not think the amount of time spent doing a task—for example, customizing the database—is worth it because the payoff isn't immediate. Thinking long range and spending some time in doing these types of tasks pays off big later.

Defining Default Values

If you find that you are entering the same information in record after record, you can define that value as a default. Then when you insert a new record, you can tell ACT! to use the default values you have defined. For example, the majority of your contacts may be in the same state. You can enter the state to use as the default.

To define default values for fields in the database, follow these steps:

1. Choose the Edit Field Defaults command.

   You see a blank record, named Field Defaults (see fig. 2.10).

2. Use the Tab key to move to the field where you want to enter a default value.

   For example, to define a default value for the State field, press Tab to move to that field.

3. Type the default.

   If most of your contacts are in Indiana, you could type IN for the State field.

4. Enter defaults for all the fields you need.

   You can enter defaults for any fields you choose. Keep in mind that you'll want to define defaults for only the most commonly used fields and values.

5. When you have completed entering the default values, choose Save.

You are returned to the contact database.

To create a record by using the default values, choose the Edit New Contact command. Choose Default. ACT! creates a record and fills in the default values you defined. Figure 2.11 shows a record where the state and Area Codes are entered automatically.

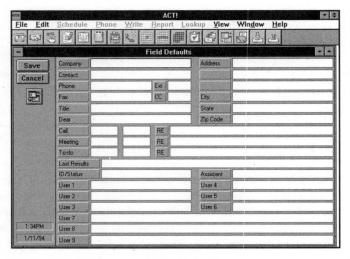

Figure 2.10. Entering field defaults.

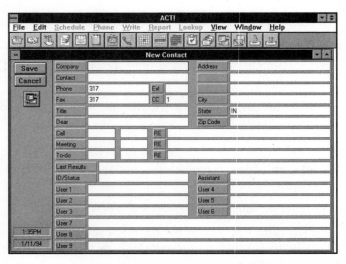

Figure 2.11. A record where default values have been entered.

Editing the Popup Menus

Popup menus appear by default for certain fields. Rather than type an entry over and over, you can select the entry from a list. For example, you can select from a list of common job titles rather than type the job title each time. ACT! creates some popup lists automatically. You can add to or modify these lists, as needed.

For information about controlling which fields have popups, see the next section.

To add to or modify a popup list, follow these steps:

1. Move to the field that has the popup you want to edit.

   For example, if you want to modify the Title popup list, move to that field.

2. Press F2 to display the popup list.

   If the field does not contain a popup, nothing appears. You can control which fields have popups. See the next section.

3. Choose the Edit button.

   When you choose the Edit button, other buttons become available in the dialog box (see fig. 2.12).

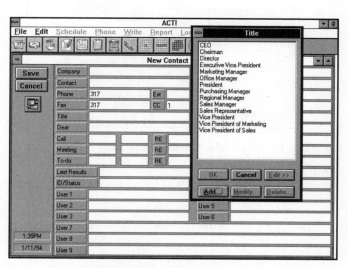

Figure 2.12. Editing a popup list.

4. Do one of the following:

✔ To add a new popup entry, choose the Add button. Type the entry and choose OK.

✔ To delete an entry, click on the entry in the list. Then choose the Delete button. When prompted, choose Yes to delete the entry.

✔ To edit an entry, click on the entry in the list. Then choose the Modify button. Edit the entry so that it reads how you want. Then choose OK.

5. When you are finished editing the popup list, choose OK.

Defining Field Attributes

You can control which fields have popups, which fields are primary fields, and more by setting field attributes. For example, you may want a popup field to appear automatically when you move to that field.

Follow these steps to set field attributes:

1. Choose the Edit Field Attributes command.

   You see the Field Attributes dialog box (see fig. 2.13).

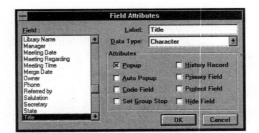

Figure 2.13. The Field Attributes dialog box.

2. In the Field list, click on the field you want to modify.

3. If you want to change the name of the field, click in the Label text box, drag across the current entry to select the text, then type the new label.

4. To change the type of data you enter in a field, display the Data Type drop-down list and select a data type:

Data Type	Description
Character	Accepts alphanumeric characters in the field.
Uppercase	Converts all alphanumeric characters typed to uppercase.
Phone number	Accepts 9 digit phone numbers. Numbers are separated as follows xxx-xxx-xxxx. You don't need to type the dashes.
Date	Accepts only dates in the format mm/dd/yy. You can type leading zeroes and ACT! will insert the slashes automatically.
Numeric	Accepts only numbers, commas, and periods in the field.
Currency	Accepts only numbers, commas, periods, dollar signs, and dashes.
0-9	Accepts only the numbers 0-9 in the field.
Time	Accepts only times in the format hh:mm. You also can type A or P.

5. Mark any of the following options:

Option	Description
Popup	When this option is marked, a popup menu is available for your use.
Auto Popup	If you want the popup menu to appear when you move to this field, mark this box. Note that this option is available only when the Popup check box (above) is marked.
Code Field	To use a code for the field, mark this box.
Set Group Stop	Assigns a group stop to this field. When you press the Group Stop key, ACT! moves to the next field with this attribute.
History Record	If this option is marked, all changes, deletions, or additions to this field are tracked in the client history.
Primary Field	If this option is marked, the field is considered a primary field. When you create a new record, you can copy the primary fields from the current record to the new record.

continues

41

Option	Description
Protect Field	Mark this field if you don't want this field to be edited or deleted.
Hide Field	Mark this field if you want to hide the field; the field will not appear in the contact screen.

6. Choose OK when you are finished completing field attributes.

Defining User Fields

If you were limited to the information in the ACT! database, the program would only be a simple Rolodex replacement. You would have no place to enter information that is critical to your business. Fortunately, ACT! is flexible and provides 15 user fields that you can define to suit your own purposes. Here are some ideas for user fields:

✔ For salespersons, create fields that indicate whether this contact is the decision maker and whether the contact has a budget. If so, create a field with the amount of the budget. Create a field for the close date.

✔ If a reporting structure for the contact is information you need, create fields for the contact's supervisor and subordinates.

✔ If you offer varying discounts for clients, create a field for the discount for the client.

✔ For all types of users, create a field or two for key conversation points. You can use these as conversation openers when you make contact with the client.

✔ For real estate brokers, create fields for the area where the client is looking for a new home, the client's budget, whether the client has a house to sell, the listing price, the range the client can afford, and more key information.

✔ For small business owners, you track several types of contacts. You might include a field for the type of business or industry and the type of contact (vendor, client, associate, and so on).

✔ If you want to set and keep objectives, create a field for current and next objectives.

To define a user field, follow these steps:

1. Move to the user field you want to define.

   You can change any of the user-defined fields (1-15) provided in the ACT! contact screens.

2. Choose the Edit Field Attributes command.

> **TIP:** *Double-click the right mouse button on a user field to display the Field Attributes dialog box.*

You see the Field Attributes dialog box.

3. Click in the Label text box, drag across the current entry to select the text, then type the new label.

4. To specify the kind of data you can enter in the field, display the Data Type drop-down list and select a data type:

Data Type	Description
Character	Accepts alphanumeric characters in the field.
Uppercase	Converts all alphanumeric characters typed to uppercase.
Phone number	Accepts 9 digit phone numbers. Numbers are separated as follows: xxx-xxx-xxxx. You don't need to type the dashes.
Date	Accepts only dates in the format mm/dd/yy. You can type leading zeroes and ACT! will insert the slashes automatically.
Numeric	Accepts only numbers, commas, and periods in the field.
Currency	Accepts only numbers, commas, periods, dollar signs, and dashes.
0-9	Accepts only the numbers 0-9 in the field.
Time	Accepts only times in the format hh:mm. You also can type A or P.

5. Mark any of the following options:

Option	Description
Popup	When this option is marked, a popup menu is available for your use.
Auto Popup	If you want the popup to appear when you move to this field, mark this box. Note that this option is available only when the Popup check box (above) is marked.
Code Field	If you want to use a code for the field, mark this box.
Set Group Stop	Assigns a group stop to this field. When you press the Group Stop key, ACT! moves to the next field with this attribute.
History Record	If this option is marked, any changes, deletions, or additions to this field will be tracked in the client history.
Primary Field	If this option is marked, the field is considered a primary field. When you create a new record, you can copy the primary fields from the current record to the new record.
Protect Field	Mark this field if you don't want this field to be edited or deleted.
Hide Field	Mark this field if you want to hide the field; the field will not appear in the contact screen.

6. Choose OK when you are finished completing field attributes.

Figure 2.14 shows a real estate contact database with customized fields.

> **TIP:** *The changes you make to the database contact screens and fields will be saved with the database. If you want to use the same contact screens for other databases, you can save the description file and then attach it to other databases. See Chapter 13 for information on using the description file.*

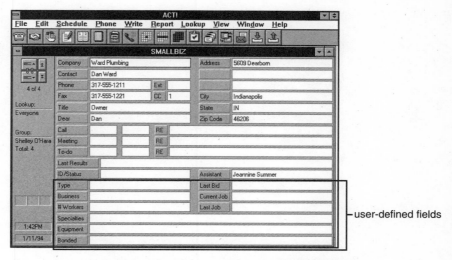

—user-defined fields

Figure 2.14. A contact database with user-defined fields.

Using the Reference Library

If you need access to a sales script during a call or access to a price or inventory list, consider using the reference library. A reference library is a word processing document that can quickly be displayed from the contact screen.

To create the reference library, type the information using the word processing program. Chapter 7 covers this program in more detail. Remember to save the file in the directory C:\ACTWIN2\DOCS. You can assign any name you like, but be sure to use the extension WPD. You can create as many library documents as you want. You can then assign the document to the appropriate contacts.

To assign a library document to a contact, display the second contact screen. In the Library field, type the file name you used when you created the file.

To display the library file, choose the View Reference Library command. You see the document you created on-screen. Figure 2.15 shows a price list.

TIP: *Press Shift+F3 to choose the View Reference Library command.*

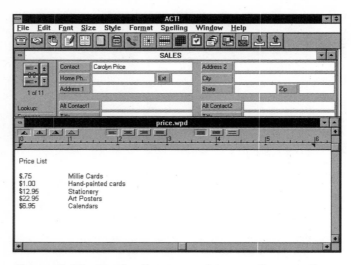

Figure 2.15. A price list created as a reference document.

To close the reference document, double-click the Control menu box in the upper-left corner of the document window.

Saving the Database

Each time you add a new record, you select Save button to save the record and the database. In addition, each time you schedule a call or meeting or make a change, the database is saved. Consequently, you don't have to worry too much about saving.

> **TIP:** *If you want to turn off autosave, see Chapter 12 on customizing ACT!*

You also can choose the File Save command to save the database, or press Ctrl+S to choose the File Save command.

If you want to save the database in another format for use with another program, see Appendix B.

If you want to save a database with a new name, choose the File Save As command. Type a new name and choose OK.

Viewing the Database

With ACT!, you cannot delete any fields in the contact database, but you can change the way you view the information in the database. For example, you may want to see a list of just phone numbers and address information. Or you may want to see all the available phone numbers for a contact. You can control what information is viewed by using the View Layout command.

> **TIP:** *To toggle between two layouts, click the* *button.*

To change the layout view, follow these steps:

1. Choose the View Layout command.

    You see a submenu of choices.

2. Select the layout you want.

Figure 2.16 shows the Rotary Index 1 layout. Figure 2.17 shows the Contact Summary layout. Figure 2.18 shows the Phone Numbers layout.

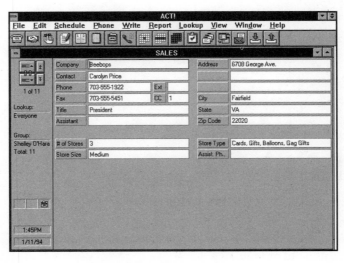

Figure 2.16. The Rotary Index 1 layout.

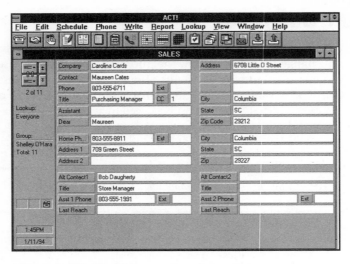

Figure 2.17. The Contact Summary layout.

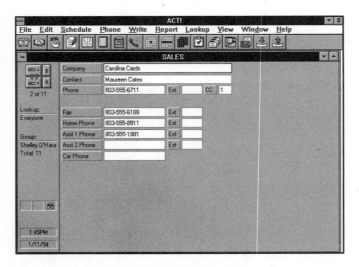

Figure 2.18. The Phone Numbers layout.

To return to the previous layout, choose the View Layout Previous command or press F6.

The View menu also enables you to view other information about a contact—for example, scheduled activities, daily calendars, and more. These options are covered later in this book.

> **TIP:** *If you need to view an on-screen calendar quickly, choose the View Calendar command or press F4. Use the scroll buttons to scroll to the appropriate month and year you want to view.*

Q&A

Do I have to complete all the fields on the contact database?

✔ You don't need to complete all the fields in a database—just the fields critical to your business. You will have to decide for yourself which fields are critical. Keep in mind that the more information you track and the more diligent you are about tracking the information, the more successful you will be.

Can I delete fields I don't need?

✔ You can't delete fields from the ACT! database. The easiest way to hide distracting fields is to change the view. For example, if you are interested only in the phone numbers for a client, change to that layout. You also can hide individual fields by modifying the field attributes. Choose the Edit Field Attributes command, click on the field, and then mark the Hide Field check box.

How do I unhide a field?

✔ Display the Field Attributes dialog box (choose the Edit Field Attributes command). Scroll through the list of field names until you see the hidden field; then click on the field. Unmark the Hide Field check box.

Can I create my own fields?

✔ ACT! provides 15 user fields that you can modify to suit your business. Move to the user field you want to change and then choose the Edit Field Attributes command. Enter a name and data type for the field. Then mark any options you want. Choose OK.

The popup menus don't contain the entries I want. How do I fix this?

✔ You can edit the popup menus to display entries pertinent to your business. To edit a popup menu, click on the field which has the popup you want to edit, and press F2. Then choose the Edit button. Choose Add and type a new entry to add an entry. To delete an entry, click on an entry and choose Delete. To modify an entry, click on the entry, choose Modify, type the new entry, and choose OK.

When I press F2 to display a popup menu, nothing happens. Why not?

✔ Some fields have no popup menus attached. You can change which fields have popup menus by setting the field attributes. Move to the field you want to add a popup to it. Then choose the Edit Field Attributes command. Mark the Popup check box.

Managing Contacts

Entering contacts is the first step in successful contact management. You also need tools to help you find, edit, sort, and list your contacts. This chapter covers these key tasks, as well as others:

- Opening a database

- Editing contact information

- Deleting a contact

- Looking up a contact

- Editing a group of contacts

- Sorting contacts

- Grouping contacts

- Printing contact information

Opening a Database

When you start ACT!, the program displays the last database on which you worked, which is convenient if you have only one database. If, however, you have more than one database or if you close the database and want to reopen it, you'll find the File Open command useful.

Follow these steps to open a database:

1. Choose the File Open command.

   You see the Open File dialog box (see fig. 3.1). All the database files (DBF) in the current directory are listed.

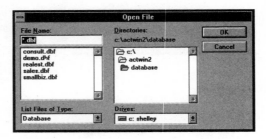

Figure 3.1. The Open File dialog box.

TIP: *Press Ctrl+O to choose the File Open command.*

---

2. In the File Name list, select the database you want to open.

   To highlight the name, you can click the file name or press Tab and then use the arrow keys.

3. Choose OK.

As a shortcut for steps 2 and 3, you can double-click the file name. ACT! opens the database on-screen.

The following checklist summarizes other key points about opening and closing a database file:

✔ If the database is stored in another directory, you can double-click the directory name in the Directories list to select the appropriate directory. ACT! displays the files in the directory. By default, ACT! stores all database files in the directory C:\ACTWIN2\DATABASE.

✔ If the database is on another drive, display the Drives drop-down list and select the drive. ACT! displays the database files on this drive.

✔ If you want to import data from another program, see Appendix B.

✔ To close a database, choose the File Close command or press Ctrl+W.

✔ You can create and use more than one database in ACT!.

Editing Contact Information

Editing contact information is easy. First, display the record you want to change. You can use the Next Record, Previous Record, First Record, and

Last Records to scroll through the records until you find the one you want. You also can search for a particular record. See the section "Looking Up a Contact" in this chapter for information on searching the database for a contact.

Next, move to the field you want to change. You can press Tab to move through the fields, or you can just click in the field you want to change. Use any of the following editing techniques to make a change:

✔ To add information, click the insertion point where you want to add information, and then type.

✔ To replace information, click to the left of the start of the entry; then hold down the mouse and drag across the entry. Doing so highlights the entry. Type a new entry to replace the one that's highlighted. You also can press the Delete or Backspace key to delete the highlighted entry.

✔ To move to the second contact screen, choose the View Layout Contact 2 command.

✔ To move text from one field to another, drag across the text. Choose the Edit Cut command. Click in the field where you want to place the text. Then choose the Edit Paste command.

✔ To copy text from one field to another, drag across the text and choose the Edit Copy command. Click in the field where you want the copy then choose the Edit Past command.

Deleting Contacts

If a contact is no longer needed, you can delete it from the database. Be sure that you no longer need any of the information. All contact information, history, and notes will be deleted. Deleting a contact is serious business, so you are warned and prompted several times to confirm the deletion.

To delete a contact, follow these steps:

1. Display the contact you want to delete.

   You can scroll through the records until you find the contact you want, or you can look up the contact. See "Looking Up a Contact."

2. Choose the Edit Delete Contact command.

TIP: *Press Ctrl+Del to choose the Edit Delete Contact command.*

You are warned that the deletion cannot be undone and asked whether you want to delete the contact or the lookup (see fig. 3.2).

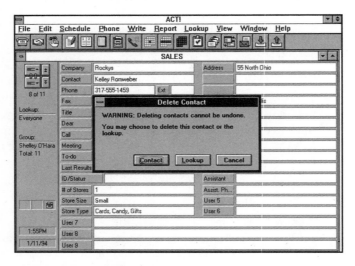

Figure 3.2. Deleting a contact.

3. Choose Contact.

   You are asked whether you are sure that you want to delete the contact.

4. Choose Yes.

5. Choose Yes.

The contact and all associated data are deleted.

Looking Up a Contact

As you add more and more contacts to your database, you don't want to waste time scrolling through looking for a particular record. Instead, you can lookup a particular contact.

Lookups provide not only a quick means to find a particular record, they also enable you to group similar contacts together. For example, you may want to group all contacts from one company together, or you may want to group contacts from one city together.

Key Concept: Understanding Lookups

A lookup provides two purposes. First, a lookup enables you to quickly find a record, rather than flip through the records as you would with a Rolodex, and display the record you need.

Second, a lookup enables you to group records. A lookup builds a group which is a subset of the records in your database—for example, all contacts in one particular city. You can use lookups to group your contacts into manageable chunks.

After the contacts are grouped, you can move from record to record in the group. If you need to make a change to a set of records, you can group them and then make the change all at once. This section discusses looking up a contact.

Performing Simple Lookups

In a simple lookup, you look up or group contacts by Company, First Name, Last Name, Phone, City, State, Zip Code, or ID/Status.

TIP: *When a contact calls, use the lookup feature to quickly find the contact. Then read the notes for the contact so that you can have an effective conversation with the caller.*

You look up a contact by following these steps:

1. Open the Lookup menu.

2. Choose the field you want to lookup and group on.

   You can choose from the following fields:

   > Company
   >
   > First Name
   >
   > Last Name
   >
   > Phone
   >
   > City

State

Zip Code

ID/Status

You see the Lookup dialog box, which prompts you to type the entry you want to match.

3. Type the entry you want to match.

For example, to find and group all contacts in Indiana, choose State from the Lookup menu and then type IN (see fig. 3.3). You can type the first character or characters in a lookup. For instance, to find all companies that start with C, type C for a Company lookup.

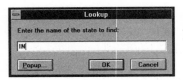

Figure 3.3. Looking up all contacts in Indiana.

TIP: *If the field has a popup menu, you can choose the Popup button in the dialog box to display a list of choices. Click the option you want, and then choose OK.*

---

4. Choose OK.

ACT! groups all similar contacts. Notice that the status bar reflects the current lookup and the number of records in the lookup group (see fig. 3.4). The total number of records appear under the group indicator.

The following checklist summarizes what you can do once you have looked up and grouped a set of records:

✔ If you are using Lookup to find a particular record, you can scroll through them to find the one you want.

✔ If you want to make a change to all the grouped records, see "Editing a Group of Records."

✔ To return to all records, choose the Lookup Everyone command.

✔ To toggle between two lookups, choose the Lookup Previous command.

✔ To display your record (the record with your company information and name), choose the Lookup My Record command.

✔ For information about displaying a priority list of activities, see Chapter 11.

✔ If no matches are found, you see an alert box saying so. Choose OK and try the lookup again.

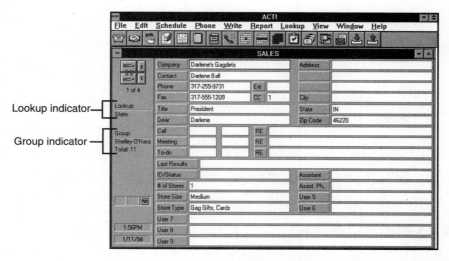

Figure 3.4. The results of looking up contacts on the State field.

Looking Up Keywords

If you can't match a record by the company name, first name, zip code, phone, city, state, or ID, you can search for a key word. For example, you can lookup and group all contacts where you use the word price list.

Follow these steps to lookup up a contact based on a key word:

1. Choose the Lookup Keyword command.

   You see the Keyword Search dialog box (see fig. 3.5). Here you type the word or words for which you are searching.

TIP: *Lookup Other is a better vehicle if just a field in the contact is needed.*

Figure 3.5. The Keyword Search dialog box.

    2. Type the word or phrase you want to find.

    You can type a word or phrase or part of a word or phrase. You also can use a wild card (*). The wild card stands for and matches any characters in that position. For example, the wild card pr* finds all words that start with *pr*. The wild card *list finds all entries that end with list. The wild card *list* finds all entries that contain the word list anywhere in the entry.

    3. Choose OK.

ACT! searches the database and groups and displays all records that contain the key word.

Performing a Custom Lookup

If a simple match or a key word match doesn't work, you can search on other fields in the database. You also may need to complete a query if you have to search on more than one field—for example, all store managers in a certain state.

Creating a Simple Query

To create a simple custom query, follow these steps:

    1. Choose the Lookup Other command.

    You see the Query screen, which is just a blank record.

    2. Move to the field, or fields, on which you want to search.

    For example, if you want to search on the Title field, click the field or press Tab until you move to the field.

    3. Type the entry you want to match.

    For example, if you want to list all store managers, type Store Manager in the Title field or use F2 for popup.

4. Enter other matching criteria.

   You can enter matching entries in other fields in the database. Figure 3.6 shows the query to find all store managers in Indiana.

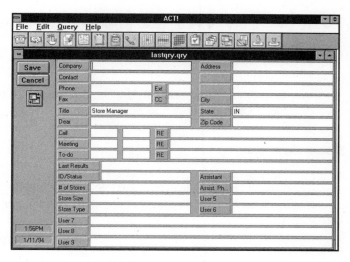

Figure 3.6. A simple custom query.

5. When you have entered the values in the fields you want to match, choose the Save button.

   You are asked whether you want to match all records or records in the active group. (See the section "Grouping Records" for more information on record groups.)

6. Choose All Contacts or Active Group and choose OK.

ACT! finds and groups all matching database records.

The following summarizes other query features:

✔ If you performed a query previously, the values for the query may appear. Choose Edit Clear to clear the values.

✔ If you click the Save button, ACT! saves the query with the name LASTQRY.QRY. Each time you create a new query and click Save, the new query is saved with this same name.

✔ To view the query as Boolean logic equations, choose the Query Convert to SmartQuery command. You see the query worded as a series of AND expressions. For more information on Boolean logic, see the following section.

✔ You can edit the query in the SmartQuery format, but sticking to the standard Query screen is easier.

✔ You also can choose Query Execute rather than Save to execute a query.

✔ To save a query with a different name (and to ensure it isn't overwritten by other new queries), choose the File Save As command. Type a new name. If you use an extension, use the extension QRY. Choose OK.

✔ You can add a custom query to the Lookup menu. See the section "Adding a Custom Lookup to the Menu."

Creating a Complex Query

A simple query works if you want an exact match—all Indiana clients or all Store Managers. When you want to match a range of values—for example, all call dates between 2/13/94 and 3/17/94, you need to work in the Smart Query view.

Follow these steps:

1. Choose the Lookup Other command.

   You see the Query screen.

2. If you want to make any exact matches, enter the values in the appropriate fields.

3. To switch to SmartQuery, choose the Query Convert to SmartQuery command.

   ACT! displays any current entries in Boolean logic and displays a SmartQuery dialog box. You can use this dialog box to add additional criteria to the search.

4. To add to the query, choose an appropriate Boolean Operator:

Operator	Description
AND	Specifies additional query. Records must meet both criteria. For example, matches all Store Managers in Indiana.
OR	Specifies additional query. A record can match either criteria. For example, matches all Store Managers or Owners.

Operator	Description
AND NOT	Matches all records that do NOT match the criteria. Records must meet both criteria. For example, match all Store Managers NOT in Indiana.
OR NOT	Matches all records that do NOT match the criteria. A record can match either criteria. For example, match all records for Store Managers or records NOT in Indiana.

5. Choose the Insert button.

6. Click on the Field Name you want to match and choose the Insert button.

7. Click on a logical operator and choose the Insert button.

8. Type the value you want to find in quotation marks (single or double). Separate the expression with parentheses.

9. Follow steps 4 through 7 to create all the criteria you want to match.

   Figure 3.7 shows a query that will find all Store Managers in Indiana with call dates after 1/4/94.

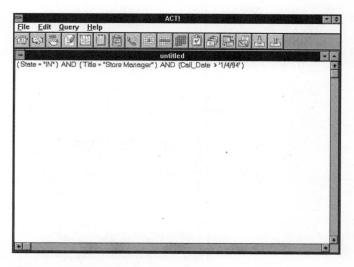

Figure 3.7. A custom query.

10. Check the query by choosing the Query Check Query command.

    If the query is formatted correctly, you see a message saying so. Click OK.

    If the query is not formatted correctly, you see an error message. Use the error message to find and fix the problem.

11. If you want to change how the query results are sorted, choose the Query Sort command and select a field to sort on. Choose OK.

12. To change the layout that is used, choose the Query Layout command. Choose a layout.

13. To save the query, choose the File Save command and type a file name. Choose OK.

14. To execute the query, choose the Query Execute command.

Adding a Custom Lookup to the Menu

If you perform the same lookups over and over, you can add the lookup to the menu. For example, suppose that you routinely lookup all store managers. You can create and save this query and then add it to the Lookup menu.

First, create and save the query as described in the previous sections. Then follow these steps:

1. Choose the Lookup Custom command.

   You see a submenu.

2. Choose the Modify Menu command.

   You see the Custom Lookup dialog box (see fig. 3.8).

Figure 3.8. The Custom Lookup dialog box.

3. Choose the Add button.

   You see the Add Custom Menu Item dialog box (see fig. 3.9).

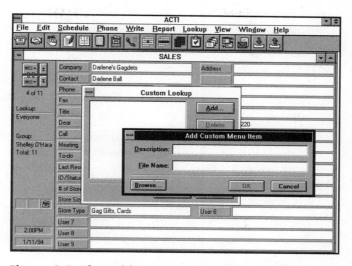

Figure 3.9. The Add Custom Menu Item dialog box.

4. In the Description text box, type the name you want to appear on the menu.

   For example, you may type Store Managers or Call Date.

5. In the File Name text box, type the name of the file.

   Type the same name you used when you saved the query.

TIP: *If you can't remember the name, click the Browse button. By default, ACT! stores all queries in the directory C:\ACTWIN2\QUERIES. You see the files in this directory. Double-click the file name, or click on the file name, then click OK.*

---

6. Click OK.

   You are returned to the Custom Lookup dialog box. The new menu item is listed in the dialog box.

7. Choose OK.

   The contact screen reappears.

The following checklist summarizes how to execute, rearrange, and delete a custom query from the menu:

✔ To execute the custom query, choose the Lookup Custom command. You should see the query name listed. Click it to select and execute the query.

✔ To delete an item from the menu, choose the Lookup Custom Modify Menu command. Click the menu item to delete, and then click the Delete button. Keep in mind that this process deletes the menu item, but does not delete the query file stored on disk.

✔ If you have several menu items that you want to rearrange, choose the Lookup Custom Modify Menu command. Click the menu item you want to change. Then click Item Up or Item Down.

✔ To separate queries by lines, choose the Lookup Custom Modify Menu command. Click the Add Line button. A line is added above the current item. (You can adjust the placement of the line by clicking on it and clicking the Item Up or Item Down button.)

Figure 3.10 shows a menu with custom queries listed.

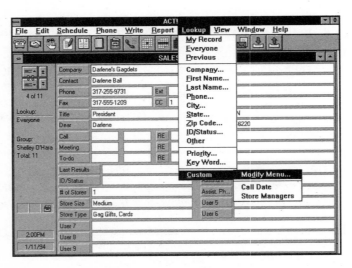

Figure 3.10. Custom queries listed on the Lookup menu.

Editing a Group of Records

In the contact database, you may have similar records—for example, several records for people that work at the same company. If you need to edit a group of records, you can do so all at once. For example, you may need to change the telephone number for a company. Rather than changing each record individually, you can change all the records at once.

To edit a group of records, you first create a lookup group that contains the records you want to edit. The previous sections describe creating lookup groups. After the group is created and the records are displayed on-screen, follow these steps to edit them:

1. Choose the Edit Current Lookup command.

    You see a blank record on-screen (see fig. 3.11).

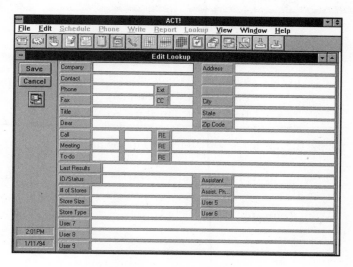

Figure 3.11. Editing a group of records.

2. Move to the field you want to change.

    You can click in the field or press Tab until you move to the field.

3. Type the new entry.

    You can change as many fields as needed. The entry you type in this field is used in all records in the lookup group.

4. Choose the Save button.

You see a message telling you that the change will affect all records in the lookup group.

To abandon the changes, click the Cancel button.

5. Choose the Yes button.

All records in the lookup group are changed.

Sorting Contacts

To sort the records in your database, you use a lookup. When you create a lookup group, ACT! sorts the database on the field you lookup and then on additional fields. The following table explains the sort order:

If you lookup...	This sort order is used...
Company	Company, Last Name, First Name
Last	Last Name, First Name, Company
City	City, Company, Last Name
State	State, City, Company
ZIP Code	Zip Code, City, Company
ID/Status	ID/Status, Company, Last Name

Follow these steps to sort all records in the database:

1. Open the Lookup menu and choose the field on which you want to sort:

   Company

   Last

   City

   State

   Zip Code

   ID/Status

2. In the dialog box that appears, press Backspace to delete any entries.

   You want to include all records, so you don't enter a value in the dialog box.

3. Click OK.

ACT! sorts the records first by the lookup field and then by the other fields listed in the preceding table. Figure 3.12 shows a contact list of records sorted by company name. See the section "Displaying a Contact List" for information on displaying this view of the database.

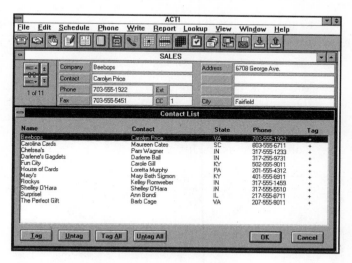

Figure 3.12. A sorted contact list.

Grouping Contacts

If you find that you are repeatedly looking up the same set of contacts, you can create lookup groups. You can add the contacts you want to this group and then quickly display all of them.

Creating a New Group

Suppose that you have clients in several states or regions. You often need to group and view the contacts by state or region when you are preparing for a sales trip. Rather than create a lookup each time you want to see this set of clients, create a group. You can create a group from a lookup or you can display all contacts and then add the ones you want to the group. You can use this method when you want to group contacts together that aren't easily grouped with a lookup—for instance, all customers with orders over a certain amount.

Follow these steps:

1. If you want to create a group from a lookup, first create the lookup.

   For instance, create a lookup for all clients in Indiana. You don't have to create a lookup. When you create the group, you can display a list of all contacts. You can then select the contacts you want to include in the group.

2. Choose the View Edit Groups command.

   You see the Edit Groups dialog box. If you have created a lookup, all the contacts in the current lookup are displayed in the Available Contact list. The Available Contact list box displays Current Lookup. If you haven't created a lookup, all contacts are listed in the Available Contact list and the list box says ALL (see fig. 3.13).

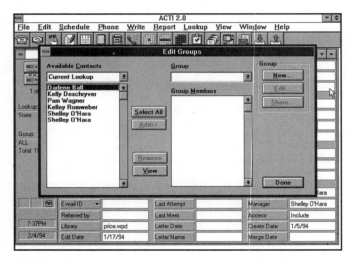

Figure 3.13. Creating an edit group.

3. Choose the New button.

   You see the New Group dialog box (see fig. 3.14).

4. Type a name in the Name text box.

   Use a name that will remind you of the contents of this edit group.

5. Type a description.

   Use a description that will help you remember why or how the contacts are grouped.

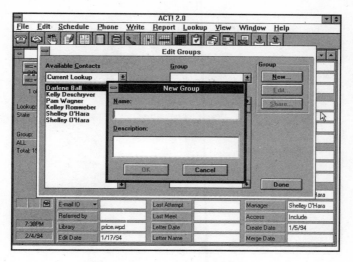

Figure 3.14. The New Group dialog box.

6. Choose OK.

   You are returned to the Edit Groups dialog box. The other buttons in the dialog box are now available. You next tell ACT! which contacts to include in this group.

7. If you want to include all the listed contacts, choose the Select All button. Then choose the Add button. To include a single contact, click on the contact name. Then choose the Add button. Do this for each contact you want to add.

   When you choose the Add button, the contacts are listed in the Group Members list box (see fig. 3.15).

TIP: *If you need to view contact information for a contact, click on the contact in the Available Contacts list and then click the View button.*

---

8. When you have finished adding all the contacts, choose the Done button.

   You are returned to the contact database screen.

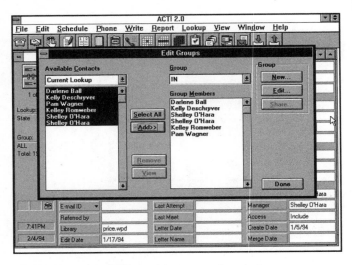

Figure 3.15. Adding contacts to the group.

Editing a Group

If you need to add or remove members from a group, you can edit the group. You can also delete groups you no longer need. Follow these steps:

1. Choose the View Edit Groups command.

   You see the Edit Groups dialog box.

2. Display the Group drop-down list and click on the group you want to edit.

   The Group drop-down list displays some predefined groups as well as any groups you have created.

3. Do any of the following:

   To remove a contact from the group, click on the contact name in the Group Members list box. Then choose the Remove button.

   To add a contact to the group, first display the name in the Available Contacts list box. You can display all contacts by displaying the drop-down list and clicking on ALL. Then click on the contact name in the Available Contacts list box. Finally, click the Add button.

   To remove a contact, click on the contact name in the Group Members list; then choose the Delete button. Choose Yes to confirm the deletion.

To edit the name of the group, choose the Edit button. You see the Edit Group dialog box (see fig. 3.16). Type a new name in the New Name text box. To change the description, edit or delete and retype the description in the Description text box. Choose the OK button.

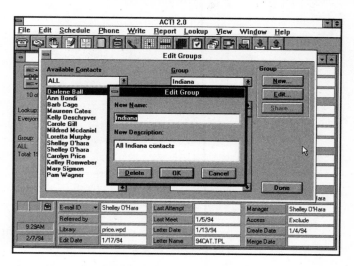

Fig. 3.16. Changing the group name.

To delete a group, choose the Edit button. You see the Edit Group dialog box. Choose the Delete button. You are prompted to confirm the deletion. Choose the Yes button.

4. To close the Edit Groups dialog box, choose the Done button.

You are returned to the contact screen.

Displaying a Group

Once you have created an edit group, you can easily and quickly display the contacts in that group. Follow these steps:

1. Choose the View Groups command.

   You see the View Group dialog box (see fig. 3.17). You see a list of groups that you have created and some predefined groups.

2. Click on the group you want displayed and choose the OK button.

   ACT! displays all contacts in that group. The Group indicator in the status bar lists the name of the selected group.

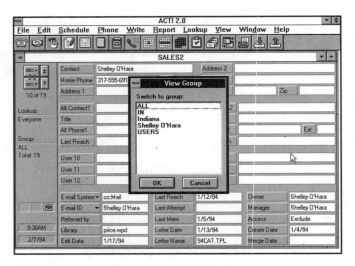

Figure 3.17. Select the group you want.

To return to all contacts, choose the View Groups command, click on the ALL group, and then choose OK.

Creating Contact Reports

In all layouts, you view the records one at a time. You also may need to view several records at once on-screen or in printed form. You can display a contact list on-screen, or you can choose to print an address book.

Displaying a Contact List

A contact list is helpful when you want to display a list of all the company names, contacts, states, and phone numbers for your contacts. You can also use the contact list to group and ungroup contacts.

TIP: *To display a list of everyone in the database, choose the Lookup Everyone command then view contact list. To display a list of only some contacts, create a lookup group for the records you want displayed. See "Looking Up a Record."*

Follow these steps to display a contact list:

1. Choose the View Contact List command. Or click the View Contact List button.

You see a contact list on-screen.

TIP: *Press F8 to choose the View Contact List command.*

---

2. Choose OK to close the contact list.

Printing an Address Book

If you want a printed copy of your contacts, you can print an address book. With an address book, you constantly have to scratch out new numbers and write in new ones. You may worry whether the address book is updated. When you use ACT! to track contact information, you don't have to worry. ACT! can quickly print an updated address book with the information you need.

TIP: *If you travel and need to take a phone list with you, print your address book before you leave. Using this report, you are sure to have the most current contact information at your fingertips.*

By default, the book is sorted by last name and the following information is printed:

Primary Address

Secondary Address

Phone Numbers

Alternate Contacts

Lines are printed between contacts. Arial 8-point type is used. You can change what is printed and control other print options.

Follow these steps to print an address book:

1. Choose the Report Print Address Book command.

    You see the ACT! Printouts dialog box (see fig. 3.18). Address Book is selected as the Printout Type.

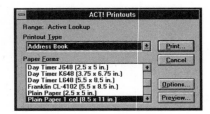

Figure 3.18. The ACT! Printouts dialog box.

2. In the Paper Forms list, select the type of paper printout you want.

You can print on either labels or regular paper. (Day Runners are useful for printing a calendar.) You also can choose to print in one or two columns.

3. To set print options, choose the Options button.

You see the Address Book Options dialog box (see fig. 3.19).

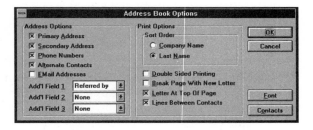

Figure 3.19. The Address Book Options dialog box.

4. Check the items you want to print; uncheck items you don't want to print:

Primary Address

Secondary Address

Phone Numbers

Alternate Contacts

E-Mail Addresses

5. If you want to print additional fields, select the field you want from the Add'l Field drop-down lists.

You can choose to print three additional fields.

6. Select a sort order: Company Name or Last Name.

   By default, the address book is sorted by last name.

7. Check or uncheck any print options you want to change:

Option	Description
Double-Sided Printing	ACT! prints on both sides of the paper. The printer needs to support this kind of printing for this option to work.
Break Page With New Letter	To print each letter of the alphabet (all A's, all B's, etc.) on a separate page, check this option.
Letter At Top Of Page	To print the letter at the top of the page, check this option.
Lines Between Contacts	ACT! prints a line between each contact. If you don't want this line, uncheck this option.

8. To control which records are printed, click the Contacts button, choose one of the following, and choose OK:

Option	Description
Active Lookup	Prints only records in the active lookup
Active Group	Prints only records in the active group
All Groups	Prints all records

9. To change the font that is used, click the Font button.

   You see the Font dialog box (see fig. 3.20).

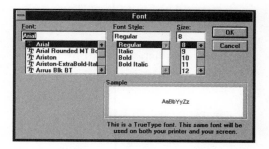

Figure 3.20. Choose a font for the address book from this dialog box.

10. In the Font list, Font Style list, and Size list, select a font, style, and size.

    For more information on fonts, see Chapter 8.

11. Choose OK.

    You are returned to the Address Book Options dialog box.

12. Choose OK.

    You are returned to the ACT! Printouts dialog box.

TIP: *To preview information in the printout, choose the Preview button. Check to be sure the information came out the way you wanted. Choose the Done button and then print the address book.*

---

13. Choose Print.

    You see the Print dialog box (see fig. 3.21).

14. Choose OK.

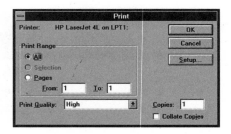

Figure 3.21. The Print dialog box.

The address book is printed. Figure 3.28 shows the first page of an address book.

For more information on printing reports, see Chapter 11.

Darlene Ball
President   Phone: 317-255-9731
Darlene's Gagdets   Fax: 317-555-1209
IN 46220

Ann Bondi
Store Manager   Phone: 217-555-8711
Surprise!   Home Phone: 217-555-0666
560 Chatty Street   Fax: 217-555-9111
Champaign, IL 61832

55 Mary Street Champaign, IL 61832

Barb Cage
Sales Manager   Phone: 207-555-9011
The Perfect Gift   Home Phone: 207-555-48884
1200 Iron Street   Fax: 207-555-4788
Williamsburg, VA 23185

809 Plum Williamsburg, VA 23185

Maureen Cates
Purchasing Manager   Phone: 803-555-6711
Carolina Cards   Home Phone: 803-555-8911
6708 Little O Street   Fax: 803-555-6188
Columbia, SC 29212

709 Green Street Columbia, SC 29227

Alt Contact1: Bob Daugherty   803-555-1991

Carole Gill
Regional Manager   Phone: 502-555-9011
Fun City   Home Phone: 502-555-4311
6709 Derby Lane   Fax: 502-555-6099
Louisville, KY 40207

7809 South River Street Lousiville, KY 40207

Alt Contact1: Patrick Yates   502-555-5011

Referred by: Kathleen Marbaugh

Figure 3.22. An address book report.

Q&A

How come I can't find the record I want? When I scroll through the records, some are missing.

> ✔ ACT! displays only the records in the current lookup group. To display all records, choose the Lookup Everyone command.

My lookup didn't work. Why not?

> ✔ If you can't find the record you need by doing a simple lookup—looking up the record on the company name, first name, last name, phone, city, state, ZIP code, or ID/Status—try a key word search or a custom search.

When I do a lookup, I get an error message that says No contacts match this request. **How do I fix this problem?**

✔ If ACT! cannot find a match, you may have made a mistake. First, be sure that you are typing the value that you want. Try redoing the lookup and be sure that you check your spelling. Second, be sure that you are working with all the records, not a subset or group.

My printer won't print.

✔ For information on setting up the printer, see Appendix A.

I can't find my database file.

✔ By default, database files are stored in the directory C:\ACTWIN2\DATABASE. If you stored the file in another drive or directory, you need to select the drive or directory in the Open File dialog box.

PART

Calls, Meetings, Mail, and Activities

Small Business Scenario

If you are a small business owner, ACT! is perfect for maintaining the many contacts in your life. Although someone in sales might store only customers, a small business owner probably keeps track of many different kinds of contacts—associates, clients, vendors, friends, and so on.

ACT! can help you manage your business better.

If you are a small business owner, you may have certain calls, meetings, and to-do items. But you also may let the day unfold and take care of calls and questions as they arise.

With ACT!, you are certain to be prepared. As you start your day, you use the daily calendar to remind you of the calls, meetings, and to-do items you need to complete for the day. You also can use the calendar to note key dates, such as project start and complete dates. ACT! reminds you of these key dates.

You make a few calls to follow up on projects but then get sidetracked on a problem. You needn't worry about missing important calls or meetings, however, because ACT! displays an alert message on-screen to remind you about upcoming calls and meetings. You can choose to snooze the alarm or make the call.

A vendor calls and you use the lookup feature to quickly find and review the caller's contact information. If this person has a question or problem, you have a record in front of you of your contact with that person. You make any additional notes so that you are up-to-date the next time the vendor calls.

In the afternoon, you need to leave the office to stop at some job sites. You print your calendar with key phone numbers so that you can make calls while you are out.

When you return to the office, you review your task list and reschedule all calls or to-dos that you didn't get to. Rescheduling is as easy as dragging and dropping the activity to another day. The next day you are prepared for another hectic day. You don't feel frantic, however, because ACT! takes care of reminding you what needs to be done.

This scenario gives you some tips on using ACT! for a small business.

Contact Screen

Information is vital to a successful business enterprise. You should therefore set up your database to contain the key information you need. In a small business, you may want to track the type of contact (vendor, clients, and so on). You may want to keep track of more personal information, such as birth dates or spouse names. You can customize the contact screen so that it is perfect for you.

The contact screen in figure S2.1 was customized for a small construction company. The owner keeps track of the type of contact, jobs, and other information.

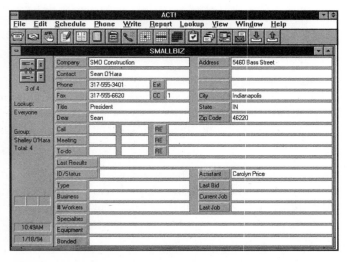

Figure S2.1. A small business contact screen.

ACT! provides a *database description file* (predesigned contact screens) that you also may want to look at. BUSINESS is designed for business use (see fig. S2.2).

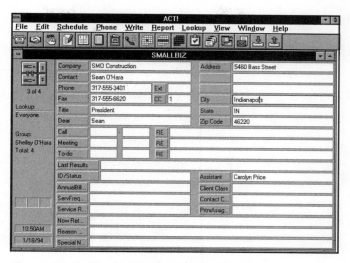

Figure S2.2. The business description file.

Customizing the database is covered in Chapter 3, "Managing Contacts." Using a description file is covered in Chapter 12, "Customizing ACT!."

If your contact database becomes too large, you may consider using two databases—one database for business and one for personal associates. If you later decide to split a contact database, you don't need to reenter all the data. You can transfer records from one database to another, as described in Chapter 13, "Maintaining the Database."

Reports

Because your database contains a variety of contacts, lookups become the key to grouping similar contacts together. For example, you may want to group and then print a directory of all vendors, or you may want to group and print an address book for all personal contacts. Lookups are covered in Chapter 3, "Managing Contacts."

As a small business owner, you may want to look at long range activities. You also may want to create a future activity report to see what activities you have planned. You can use the monthly calendar to view a monthly overview of scheduled activities (see fig. S2.3).

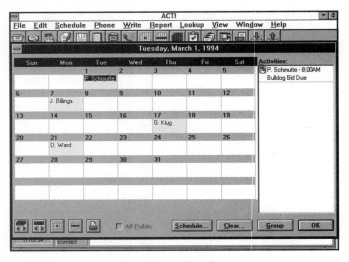

Figure S2.3. The monthly calendar.

Prioritizing your activities is critical. If you can only get so much done a day, you should concentrate on the high-priority activities. Using the task list, you can view only high-priority tasks, as described in Chapter 5, "Managing Your Schedule."

Correspondence

If you submit proposals or quotes, you can use ACT!'s word processing program to create the document. The word processing program includes editing and formatting features that make it easy to create a polished looking document.

In addition, you can create letters, memos, or fax cover sheets quickly. If you have a fax/modem installed in your computer, you can even fax the documents right from your computer.

Scheduling Your Day

Keeping track of your contacts is one key to a successful business. The other key is tracking what needs to be done. Whom do you need to call? Where are you in the sales process? What meetings have you set up? What's on your to-do list? ACT! can help you schedule your day so that you know exactly what needs to be done.

This chapter covers the following topics:

- Scheduling calls
- Scheduling meetings
- Creating a to-do list

Time-Management Tip

Effective time management means making choices about how you spend your time. To make effective choices, you need to know how you spend your time and how your time is best spent.

Scheduling Calls

If you are a salesperson, much of your time is probably spent making calls. Tracking who you have called, who you are supposed to call, who you actually reached, who you need to call back, and so on can be a nightmare. If you write down all the calls, you need to write down the name and find the appropriate number. If you don't make the call that day, you need to rewrite the entry on the next day.

When you use ACT!, tracking all your calls is easy. You have all pertinent phone numbers readily available. You also can quickly record the status of your call—whether you completed or attempted the call. And you can update any other pertinent information—for example, the Last Results field.

Calls, Meetings, and Activities

The benefit of using ACT! to schedule calls, meetings, and activities is that ACT! creates two links. First, the call, meeting, or activity is linked to the contact. When you complete and clear the activity, ACT! makes a notation in the contact history so that you can keep a record of contact interaction.

Second, calls, meetings, and activities are linked to the calendar so that you can easily display all the tasks you need to accomplish in one day, week, or month.

Scheduling a Call

In your business, you may make 20 to 40 calls a day. To remind yourself whom you need to call and when, use ACT! to schedule the calls. To schedule a call, follow these steps:

1. Display the contact whom you want to call.

   For help on finding contacts, see Chapter 3. You should see the contact record on-screen.

2. Choose the Schedule Call command or click the Schedule call button.

   You see an on-screen calendar with a dialog box behind the calendar (see fig. 4.1). You first select the date and time for the call.

3. Click the date on which you want to make the call.

   If the date you want isn't in the current month or current year, use the scroll buttons at the bottom of the calendar. The first set of scroll buttons scrolls through the months. The second set of scroll buttons scrolls the year.

4. Choose OK.

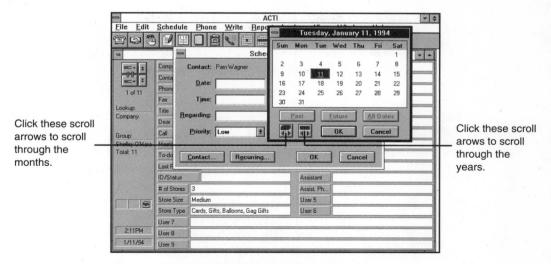

Click these scroll arrows to scroll through the months.

Click these scroll arows to scroll through the years.

Figure 4.1. Selecting the date for the call.

When you select the date and choose OK, ACT! displays a date book so that you can select the time (see fig. 4.2).

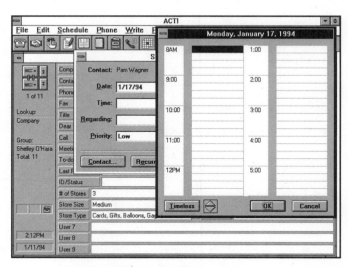

Figure 4.2. Selecting the time for the call.

5. Click on the time for the call. If you can make the call at any time, click the Timeless button.

You can use the scroll arrows to display earlier or later times than the times shown. If you want to block off an amount of time for the call, click at the beginning of the call and drag down until you highlight enough time for the call, then release the mouse button.

6. Choose OK.

   You see the RE popup dialog box (see fig. 4.3).

7. If you see an item that describes the purpose of the call, click on the item, then choose OK. If you don't want to use one of the popup values, click Cancel. Then type the purpose for the call manually in the Regarding text box.

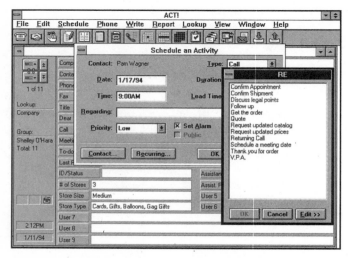

Figure 4.3. Entering the purpose of the call.

TIP: *You can edit the popup menu to display the options you want. Chapter 2 covers editing a popup menu.*

You see the Schedule an Activity dialog box. The date, time, duration, and purpose are completed (see fig. 4.4).

Figure 4.4. The Schedule an Activity dialog box.

8. If you want to change the priority of the call, display the drop-down list and select a new priority.

   The default priority is Low.

9. To specify a different duration, delete the current duration and type a new value.

   The default duration is either 15 minutes or the amount of time you dragged across when you selected the time. You can press F2 to display the Duration popup.

TIP: *You can set a different default duration and lead time. See Chapter 12 on customizing.*

---

10. If you want to specify a lead time for the call, type the needed lead time in the Lead Time text box.

    The default is 0. You can press F2 to display the Lead Time popup.

11. If you don't want ACT! to use an alarm, uncheck the Set Alarm check box.

    For more information on alarms, see the section "Responding to an Alarm."

12. If you want to send an e-mail message, check the Send E-mail check box.

TIP: *If you want to schedule an activity for another contact, click the Contact button and then click on the contact name and choose OK.*

---

13. Choose OK.

The call is scheduled. An entry is made to the activity list, and an icon appears on the contact record. The call is also noted in the Call area of the contact record (see fig. 4.5).

Chapter 6 covers e-mail in more detail.

Scheduling Recurring Calls

If you routinely make a call to a contact on a set basis—perhaps monthly or weekly—you can set up a recurring call. Follow the steps in the preceding section to enter the start date, time, duration, purpose, and priority of the call. Before you choose OK to schedule the call, choose the Recurring button. You see the Recurring Activity dialog box (see fig. 4.6).

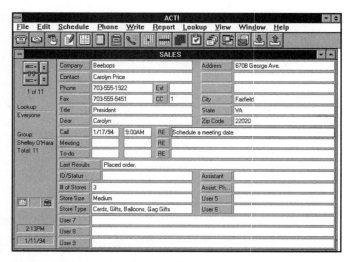

Figure 4.5. A scheduled call.

> **CAUTION:** *Keep in mind that recurring activities scheduled over long periods with frequent reccurences may become more of a nuisance than a help. You will be frequently reminded of them. If you travel a lot and are away from your computer, you should also reconsider scheduling this type of activity.*

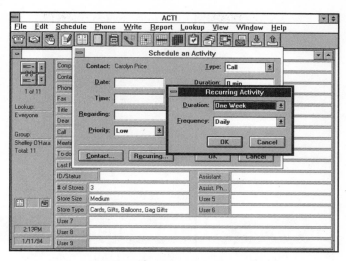

Figure 4.6. Scheduling a recurring activity.

Display the Duration drop-down list and select how long you want to set up the recurring call. Display the Frequency drop-down list and select how often you want to schedule the call. Choose OK.

Keeping a Call History

Life would be great if everyone you called was available the first time you called. More than likely, you often will need to leave a message or call back. You can keep a history of the calls you made.

Note that when you keep a call history, the call is still scheduled. To clear a scheduled call, see the next section.

TIP: *To display a quick list of all the pertinent phone calls for a contact, choose the Phone List command. You see all of the phone numbers for the contact. Click Cancel to close the dialog box. (You can use this dialog box to make the phone call by using your computer. See the section "Dialing Automatically" for more information.)*

To keep a call history, follow these steps:

1. Choose the Phone Call History command.

You see the Call History dialog box (see fig. 4.7).

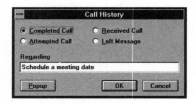

Figure 4.7. The Call History dialog box.

2. Choose one of the following options:

Option	Description
Completed Call	Records the call as completed in contact history; retains the scheduled call.
Attempted Call	Records the call as attempted in contact history and retains the scheduled call.
Received Call	Records that you received a call and retains the scheduled call.
Left Message	Records that you left a message and keeps the scheduled call.

3. If you want to make a note about what the call was regarding, type it in the Regarding text box. Or click the Popup button, select an option from the list, and choose OK.

4. Choose OK.

The option you selected is entered in the contact history. For more information on viewing client histories, see Chapter 5.

Clearing a Call

When you want to retain the scheduled call, but keep a history of call attempts, use the Call History. When you want to clear the call and enter a note in the client history, use the Clear Call command, as described in this section.

> **NOTE:** *When you use ACT! to make the call, the history is maintained automatically. You need to track only manual calls.*

To clear a call, follow these steps:

1. Choose the Clear Call command.

   You see the Clear Call dialog box (see fig. 4.8).

Figure 4.8. Clearing a call.

2. Choose one of the following options:

Option	Description
Completed Call	Records the call as completed in contact history and clears the scheduled call.
Attempted Call	Records the call as attempted in contact history and clears the scheduled call.
Received Call	Records that you received a call and clears the scheduled call.
Left Message	Records that you left a message and clears the scheduled call.
Erase Call	Erases the call and makes no entry in the contact history.

3. Choose OK.

The appropriate entry is made in the contact history. The call is deleted from the activity list, and ACT! updates the Last Reach and Last Attempt dates, as appropriate.

Dialing Automatically

If you have a modem installed and if you have a telephone connected to the modem line, you can make phone calls by using the Phone menu. First, you need to set up your modem. Appendix A covers setting up a modem. You then can make the call. ACT! calls the number in the company phone number field.

To make a call, follow these steps:

1. Open the Phone menu.

2. Choose the appropriate option:

Option	Description
Local	Choose for local calls.
Long Distance	Choose if the call is long distance.
International	Choose if the call is international.
Alternate Access	Choose if you use a special long distance service or number.

ACT! calls the number.

3. Choose OK.

If the person answers, you can pick up your extension. ACT! displays the Phone dialog box. You can choose the following:

Option	Description
Yes	Choose Yes if the call was completed. ACT! adds the call to the contact history and updates the date in the Last Reach field.
Attempted	Choose this option if you attempted the call, but did not reach the contact. ACT! adds this to the contact history and updates the Last Attempt field.
Redial	If you don't get through the first time, choose this option to redial the number.
Timer	To time the call, click this button. See the section "Timing a Call."
Cancel	To cancel the call, choose this button.

> **TIP:** *If you want to dial another number other than the company phone number, choose the Phone List command or click the Phone List button.*
>
>
>
> *Click on the number you want to call or type the number in the Enter manually text box. Then choose OK.*

> **TIP:** *You can dial a number directly from the phone list. Display the phone list by choosing the Phone List command. Then click on the number you want to dial and choose OK.*

Scheduling Meetings

You schedule and clear meetings the same way you schedule and clear calls. There are some slight variations in the process.

> ## Time-Management Tip
> *To save time, consider combining two activities. For example, if you are working on a project with a co-worker, discuss the project at lunch.*

Scheduling a Meeting

Use ACT! to schedule and track your meetings. Follow these steps:

1. Display the contact with whom you are meeting.

   If the meeting does not involve any of your contacts, display your own record ("My Record") and schedule the meeting with this contact.

2. Choose the Schedule Meeting command or click the Schedule Meeting button.

   You see an on-screen calendar with a dialog box behind the calendar. You first select the date and time for the meeting.

3. Click on the meeting date.

   If the date you want isn't in the current month or current year, you can use the scroll buttons at the bottom of the calendar. The first set of scroll buttons scrolls through the months. The second set of scroll buttons scrolls the year.

4. Choose OK.

When you select the date and choose OK, ACT! displays a date book so that you can select the time.

5. Click and hold down the mouse button at the meeting starting time; drag down to block out enough time for the meeting. Then release the mouse button.

If you hold the meeting at any time, click the Timeless button.

You can use the scroll arrows to display earlier or later times than the ones shown.

6. Choose OK.

You see the RE popup dialog box for meetings (see fig. 4.9).

7. If you see an item that describes the purpose of the meeting, click the item, and then choose OK. If you don't want to use one of the popup values, click Cancel. Then, in the Regarding text box, type the purpose for the meeting.

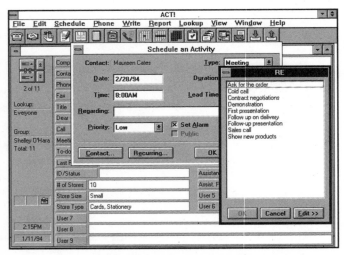

Figure 4.9. Entering the purpose of the meeting.

TIP: *You can edit the popup menu to display the options you want. Chapter 2 covers editing a popup menu.*

You see the Schedule an Activity dialog box. The date, time, duration, and purpose are completed.

8. If you want to change the priority of the meeting, display the drop-down list and select a different priority.

   The default priority is Low.

9. If you want to specify a different duration, delete the current duration and type a new value.

   The default duration is 15 minutes or the amount of time you dragged across when you selected the time.

TIP: *You can set a different default duration and lead time. See Chapter 12 on customizing.*

---

10. If you want to specify a lead time for the meeting, type the lead time needed in the Lead Time text box.

    The default is 30.

11. If you don't want ACT! to use an alarm, uncheck the Set Alarm check box.

    For more information on alarms, see the section "Responding to an Alarm."

TIP: *You can also disable all alarms. See Chapter 12 on customizing ACT!.*

---

12. If you want to send an e-mail message, check the Send E-mail check box.

    Chapter 6 covers e-mail in more detail.

13. Choose OK.

The meeting is scheduled and listed in the calendar and on the contact screen (see fig. 4.10).

Scheduling Recurring Meetings

Just as you can set recurring calls, you can similarly set recurring meetings. For instance, you may have a staff meeting once a week or once a month. Use ACT! to schedule these meetings.

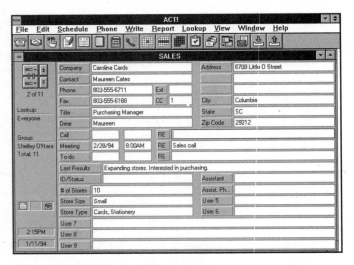

Figure 4.10. A scheduled meeting.

To schedule a recurring meeting, complete the Schedule an Activity dialog box, as described. Enter the start date, time, duration, purpose, and priority of the meeting. Before you choose OK to schedule the meeting, choose the Recurring button.

In the Recurring dialog box, display the Duration drop-down list and select how long you want to set up the recurring meeting. Display the Frequency drop-down list and select how often you want to schedule the meeting. Choose OK.

Clearing a Meeting

To clear a meeting on your activity list, follow these steps:

1. Choose the Clear Meeting command.

   You see a prompt that asks you whether the meeting was held.

2. Choose Yes if you held the meeting, No if you didn't.

The meeting is cleared from the activity list. An entry is made to the contact history for the meeting. ACT! updates the Last Meet date in the second contact screen.

Responding to an Alarm

When you check the Set Alarm check box in the Schedule an Activity dialog box, ACT! alerts you when you have calls or meetings waiting. You hear a beep and see the Critical Alarm dialog box (see fig. 4.11).

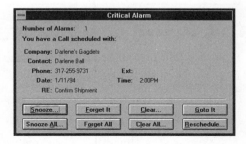

Figure 4.11. Responding to an alarm.

Choose one of the following options:

Option	Description
Snooze	Select to postpone the alarm. You see a dialog box; select the amount of time you want to postpone the alarm (5 Minutes, 10 Minutes, 20 Minutes, 30 Minutes, 1 Hour, 90 Minutes, 4 Hours, 1 Day).
Snooze All	Select to postpone alerting all activities. Select the amount of time to postpone in the Snooze dialog box (same options as for Snooze).
Forget It	Select if you want to forget about the activity and don't want to be reminded again.
Forget All	Select if you want to forget about all activities.
Clear	To clear the activity, select this option. You see the Clear Call or Clear Meeting dialog box. Select the appropriate option. See the section on "Clearing Calls" and "Clearing Meetings."
Clear All	Select if you want to clear all activities. Then select how you want to clear each activity.
Goto it	Select to display the contact for whom the call or meeting is scheduled.
Reschedule	Select to reschedule the activity. You see the Modify an Activity dialog box. See the section "Editing a Call or Meeting."

Time-Management Tip

If an item remains on your activity list for more than a couple of days, make sure that you really need to complete that item. If you do, make it a priority. If you don't, forget about it.

Timing a Call, Activity, or Meeting

If you bill by the hour or need to track the time of a call for another reason, you can use the timer. You can use the timer to time a call, meeting, or activity. Follow these steps to time an event:

1. Choose the Edit Start Timer command.

   You see the Timer dialog box (see fig. 4.12).

Figure 4.12. Timing an event.

TIP: *Press Shift+F4 to choose the Edit Start Timer command.*

---

2. Select what you want to time:

   Call

   Meeting

   To-do

   Other

3. In the RE text box, type a note to remind you what activity you are timing.

   You can click the Popup button to display a popup list of choices. Click the item you want in the list, and then click OK.

4. Choose OK.

You see an Elapsed Time dialog box at the bottom of the contact screen (see fig. 4.13). This dialog box records the amount of time spent, until you pause, restart, or stop the timer.

TIP: *If you need to pause or restart the timer, choose the appropriate button. If you click the Pause button, click the Resume button to resume timing.*

---

5. When the activity is completed, choose the Stop button.

The amount of time will be recorded in the client history. See Chapter 5 for information on viewing and modifying the client history.

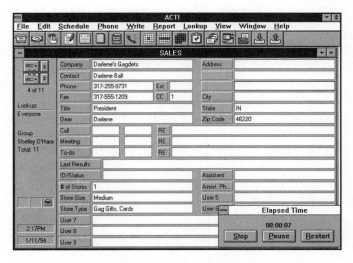

Figure 4.13. The Elapsed Time dialog box.

Handling Schedule Conflicts

When you schedule two activities at the same time, ACT! alerts you that a schedule conflict exists. You see the Conflict dialog box (see fig. 4.14). Choose Accept to accept the conflict, or choose Reschedule and select another date or time.

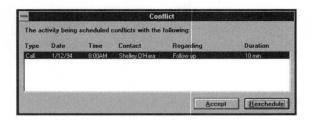

Figure 4.14. Resolving schedule conflicts.

Creating a To Do List

Besides making calls and attending meetings, you probably need to complete other activities during the day. For example, you may need to send a fax, memo, or letter. You may need to send a proposal or quote. You can create and manage your to-do list with ACT!

Time-Management Tip

Keeping a to-do list helps you identify which projects you can delegate. Be fair when you delegate. Don't wait until the last minute. Identify and hand-off any tasks that would be best handled by another person.

Scheduling an Activity

If you have the hang of scheduling a meeting or call, you quickly can learn how to schedule an activity. The processes are similar. To schedule an activity, follow these steps:

1. If the activity is related to a particular contact, display that contact. If the activity is not related to a contact, display your record.

   Chapters 2 and 3 explain how to find a particular record.

2. Choose the Schedule To-do command or click the Schedule To-do button.

   You see an on-screen calendar with a dialog box behind the calendar. You first select the date and time for the to-do activity.

3. Click the date on which you plan to complete the activity.

If the date you want isn't in the current month or current year, use the scroll buttons at the bottom of the calendar. The first set of scroll buttons scrolls the months. The second set of scroll buttons scrolls the year.

4. Choose OK.

   You see the RE popup dialog box (see fig. 4.15).

5. If you see an appropriate to-do activity, click on it and then choose OK. If you don't want to use one of the popup values, click Cancel. Then manually type the activity in the Regarding text box.

TIP: *You can edit the popup menu to display the options you want. Chapter 2 covers editing a popup menu.*

You see the Schedule an Activity dialog box. The date and regarding entries are completed. Time is set to None.

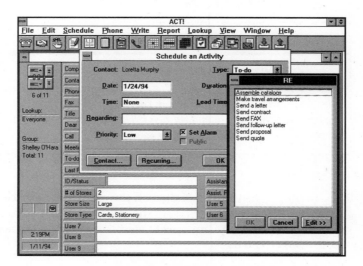

Figure 4.15. Select the to-do activity you want.

6. If you want to change the priority of the to-do, display the drop-down list and select a different priority.

   The default priority is Low.

7. To set a duration for the activity, type the value in the Duration text box.

The default duration is 0.

8. If you want to specify a lead time for the to-do, type the lead time needed in the Lead Time text box.

The default is 0.

9. If you don't want ACT! to use an alarm, uncheck the Set Alarm check box.

For more information on alarms, see the section "Responding to an Alarm." For information on disabling alarms, see Chapter 12.

10. If you want to send a e-mail message, check the Send E-mail check box.

Chapter 6 covers e-mail in more detail.

TIP: *To schedule a recurring activity, choose the Recurring button. Then select a duration and frequency for the activity and choose OK.*

Time-Management Tip

Making a to-do list is beneficial because it ensures that you remember the tasks you want to accomplish. You can prioritize the list so that you are sure to complete the most important tasks. The list can also be used as a progress report—to see how much you have completed.

---

11. Choose OK.

The activity is scheduled and noted on the contact screen (see fig. 4.16). An entry for the activity is made in the activity and task list and on the calendar. Chapter 5 explains how to view and maintain the activity and task list and calendars.

Clearing an Activity

When you complete an activity, clear it using ACT! so that you have a record of when the task was completed. Follow these steps to clear an activity:

1. Choose the Clear To-do command.

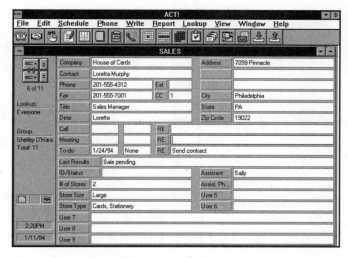

Figure 4.16. A scheduled meeting.

You see a message asking whether the to-do item was completed.

2. Choose Yes if you completed the task, No if you didn't.

The activity is cleared from the activity list. An entry is made to the contact history for the activity.

> **NOTE:** *If you have more than one to-do item scheduled, ACT! clears the current to-do item. You may not know which is current. In this case, use the Activity list to select and clear the appropriate to-do list item. See Chapter 5 for information on the Activity list.*

Time-Management Tip

If you make a to-do list, cross off the items you complete. Crossing off an item helps you keep track of what you have finished and what you still need to do and also gives you a sense of accomplishment.

Q&A

How can I tell which calls, meetings, and activities I've scheduled?

✔ You can use either the activity or the task list to keep track of what tasks and activities you have scheduled. Chapter 5 explains these features.

If I scheduled a call for the wrong contact, how can I undo it?

✔ If you accidentally scheduled a call or meeting for the wrong contact, you can delete the call or meeting from the contact history, activity list, and task list. See Chapter 5.

How come I get an error message when I try to use the Phone option?

✔ You must have a modem installed and set up properly for these options to work. If you don't have a modem, you cannot make calls using the Phone menu. Also, other programs may have the modem tied up.

How do I schedule a call, meeting, or activity that doesn't pertain to any of my contacts?

✔ When you have a call, meeting, or activity that doesn't relate to any of your contacts, schedule the item on your record. Remember that when you first set up the database, you created a record with your name and contact information. This record is created for this purpose—so that you can schedule non-contact related activities.

Managing Your Schedule

The payoff of entering your contacts and scheduling your calls, meetings, and to-do lists with ACT! is the ease with which you can view and manage the schedule. You can begin your day with a complete list of calls, meetings, and tasks you need to accomplish. You don't need to worry about where you need to start. ACT! manages your schedule for you.

This chapter covers the following topics:

- Viewing the contact history

- Working with the activity list

- Viewing activity totals

- Using the task list

- Looking up tasks by priority

- Viewing and printing calendars

Viewing the Contact History

Your contact history is a record of your calls, meetings, and projects with a contact. The history reminds you what you have done, where you are in the sales process, and what needs to be done. All this information is recorded when you use ACT! to schedule and clear your activities.

You can display the contact history easily. If necessary, you can edit the history—for example, delete older entries. The following sections describe these editing tasks.

Displaying the Contact History

As you talk on the phone with a contact, you may want to review the calls, meetings, and activities associated with the contact. Alternatively, you may want to refresh your memory by viewing the contact history before you make a call.

To display the contact history, follow these steps:

1. Display the desired contact.

   Chapter 2 explains how to scroll through the contacts. If you want to look up a particular contact, see Chapter 3.

2. Choose the View History command or click the View History button.

You see the history for the contact (see fig. 5.1). You see the date, time, kind of event (call, meeting, or to-do) for each event. A description of the event also appears. (The entry you made in the Regarding text box when you scheduled the activity is used for the description.) The status of the event also is stated—that is, whether the call was made, the meeting was held, and so on.

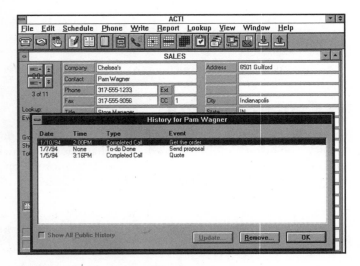

Figure 5.1. A contact history.

> **TIP:** *Press Shift+F9 to choose the View History command.*

After you finish reviewing the history, you can choose the OK button to close the history window.

Editing the Contact History

You may occasionally need to edit the contact history. Perhaps you made an entry by mistake, or perhaps including an event you recorded isn't necessary in the contact history. You can remove events from the contact history by following these steps:

1. Click on the event you want to remove.

   The event should be highlighted.

2. Choose the Remove button.

   You see an alert box asking you to confirm the change (see fig. 5.2).

Figure 5.2. Confirm that you want to remove the item from the history.

3. Choose Yes to remove the item.

   The item is removed.

4. Choose OK to close the history window.

> **TIP:** *You can print a history summary. For information on creating reports, see Chapter 11.*

Working with the Activity List

Tracking what you need to do when is easy when you use ACT! to schedule the to-do list items. ACT! compiles a to-do list for each contact. You can review and update the activity list as you work.

Displaying the Activity List

Follow these steps to display the scheduled activities for a contact:

1. Display the contact you want.

   Chapter 2, "Setting Up a Contact Database," explains how to scroll through the contacts. If you want to look up a particular contact, see Chapter 3, "Managing Contacts."

2. Choose the View Activities command or click the View Activities button.

You see the activities for the contact (see fig. 5.3). The kind of activity, scheduled date and time, purpose, duration, lead time, and priority are listed in the activity window.

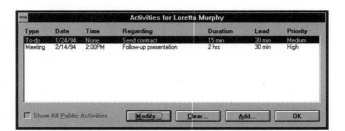

Figure 5.3. Scheduled activities.

TIP: *Press Alt+F9 to choose the View Activities command.*

After you finish reviewing the activities, choose OK to close the window.

If you need a report of all activities for all contacts, you can create an activity report. You can create a report that summarizes all future activities for all contacts or all completed activities. Chapter 11, "Creating Form Letters and Templates," covers reports in greater detail.

If you want to see a list of all scheduled activities for the current day or a range of dates, use the task list. See the section, "Using the Task List," later in this chapter.

Editing the Activity List

You can update the activity list—add new items, clear completed items, or modify scheduled items. To add a new item, choose the Add button. You see an on-screen calendar and the Schedule an Activity dialog box. Schedule the activity as described in Chapter 4, "Scheduling Your Day."

To change an item, click the item you want to modify, and then choose the Modify button. You see the Modify an Activity dialog box (see fig. 5.4). Make all changes to the date, time, duration, lead time, priority, and purpose. Then choose OK.

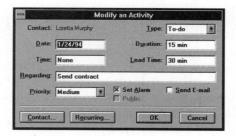

Figure 5.4. The Modify an Activity dialog box.

To clear an item, click on the item in the activity list, and then choose the Clear button. You see an appropriate Clear dialog box; the dialog box varies, depending on the kind of activity. Choose the option you want. See Chapter 4, "Scheduling Your Day," for more information on clearing calls, meetings, and activities.

After you finish editing the activity list, choose the OK button to close the activity window.

Time-Management Tip

At the end of the day, review your task list. Check off all completed tasks. Move all unfinished tasks to the next day's list. Ask yourself if you spent your time wisely today.

Viewing Activity Totals

To view the total number of activities performed (calls completed, calls attempted, meetings held, and letters sent), choose the View Totals command or press Ctrl+F9. Figure 5.5 shows the View Totals window.

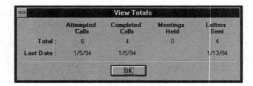

Figure 5.5. Viewing the totals.

Using the Task List

If you individually check each contact screen for scheduled activities, you waste a lot of time checking and trying to remember which contacts have scheduled activities. ACT! doesn't make you do this. When you want an overview of all scheduled activities, you can use the task list.

The task list can display the calls, meetings, and to-do items for the current date, tomorrow, or a range of dates. You can choose to display all items or only items with a certain priority.

Besides viewing the task list, you also can make changes—for example, clear items you have completed.

Viewing the Task List

To see an overview of the entire day's activities, display the task list. Choose the View Task List command or click the View Task List button.

You see the scheduled tasks for the current day (see fig. 5.6). By default, the activities for the current day are listed, and items of all priorities and all types are listed. You can change the information that ACT! displays.

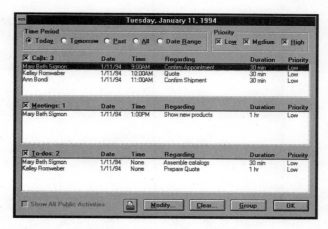

Figure 5.6. Scheduled tasks for the current day.

TIP: *Press F7 to choose the View Task List command.*

To change what is displayed, take any of the following actions:

✔ To view the task list for another day, choose another time period. You can choose Today (the default), Tomorrow, Past, All, or a Date Range. When you select Date Range, you see a calendar on-screen. Click on the first date you want to include. Hold down the mouse button and drag across the dates you want to include. Then release the mouse button. All activities within the selected dates are listed.

✔ To list items by priority, check or uncheck the Priority check boxes. When the box is checked, items of the box's priority are listed. When the box is unchecked, items of the box's priority are not listed. To include only high priority check boxes, for example, uncheck Low and Medium.

✔ To display only certain types of activities, check or uncheck the Calls, Meetings, or To-dos check boxes. Again, when a box is checked, the checked activity is included. When the box is unchecked, the activity is omitted.

Figure 5.7 shows a task list for a range of dates. Figure 5.8 shows only high priority projects listed.

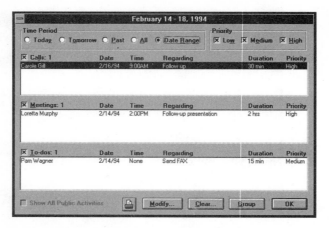

Figure 5.7. A task list for the dates February 14 through 18.

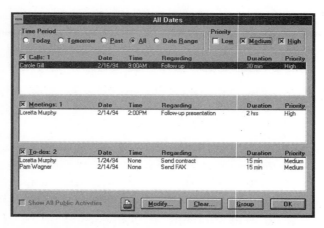

**Figure 5.8. A task list showing only medium and high priority
projects.**

Editing the Task List

Just as you should use ACT! to schedule calls, meetings, and to-dos, you also
should use ACT! to track what you have completed. If you are working from
the task list, you can use it to clear finished projects. You also can modify
scheduled items.

To change an item, click on the item you want to modify and choose
the Modify button. You see the Modify an Activity dialog box. Make all
changes to the date, time, duration, lead time, priority, and purpose. Then
choose OK.

To clear an item, click on the item in the task list and choose the Clear button. Make the appropriate choice in the Clear dialog box. (Keep in mind that the dialog box varies depending on the kind of activity. Chapter 4 covers clearing items in more detail.)

> **TIP:** *Choose the Group button to group all contacts with scheduled activities. Using this option makes grouping and displaying the appropriate contact records for your day an easy task.*

After you finish editing the task list, choose the OK button to close the task list.

> **TIP:** *If you want a hard copy of the task list, you can print it. See Chapter 11 for information about creating and printing reports.*

Looking Up Tasks by Priority

When you schedule an activity (call, meeting, or to-do), you assign a priority. Your High priority projects are, of course, very important. ACT! provides a way to lookup and group contacts based on priority projects assigned to the contact. Chapter 3 covers lookups in greater detail.

To lookup based on priority, follow these steps:

1. Choose the Lookup Priority command.

   You see the Lookup Priority dialog box (see fig. 5.9).

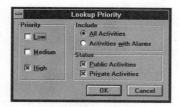

Figure 5.9. Looking up contacts based on priority activities.

2. In the Priority area, check the priority you want to look up (Low, Medium, or High).

   By default, only the High check box is checked.

3. If you want to include only activities with alarms, choose the Activities with Alarms option button.

   By default, all activities are looked up.

4. If you use ACT! on a network, choose a status: Public Activities or Private Activities.

5. Choose OK.

ACT! groups and displays all contacts with scheduled activities matching the priority, alarm status, and public/private status you entered.

Viewing Calendars

Besides the preceding ways to manage and view your schedule, you also can view a calendar view, similar to a daybook. You can view a day, week, or month view of your calendar. You can help manage the flow of your schedule by using the calendars. Is one day overloaded? What about your vacation week? How is the next month shaping up?

You can edit the calendar entries—reschedule an entry, clear an entry, group contacts. And if you want a printed version of your calendar, you can create one easily.

Displaying Day, Week, or Month Views

To display a calendar view of your schedule, follow these steps:

1. Open the View menu.

   You see a list of View commands.

2. Choose one of the following: Day, Week, or Month.

   You also can click the Day View, Week View, or Month View buttons.

Figures 5.10, 5.11, and 5.12 show a day view, a week view, and a month view, respectively.

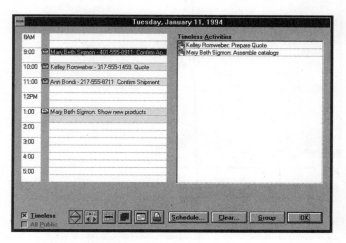

Figure 5.10. A day view.

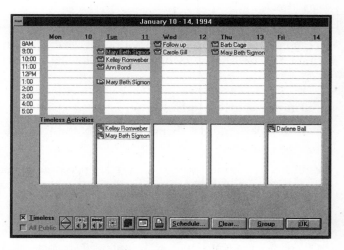

Figure 5.11. A week view.

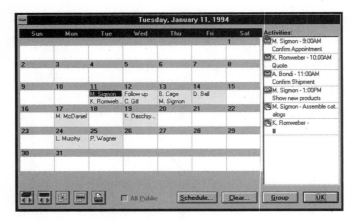

Figure 5.12. A month view.

> **TIP:** *Press Shift+F5 for the day view, F3 for the week view, and F5 for the month view.*

You can use the buttons along the bottom of the calendar to display a different view or date, as described in the following checklist:

- ✔ For day and week views, uncheck the Timeless check box to hide all Timeless activities (activities not assigned a particular time).

- ✔ In day view, you can change the time of the activity by dragging it to a new time.

- ✔ In week or month view, you can rearrange your schedule. Click on the entry you want to move and then drag it to the new day.

In the contact list, all contacts are tagged by default. When a contact is tagged, it is included in the lookup group. To untag a contact, click on it and then click the Untag button. To untag all contacts, click on the Untag All button. To tag a contact, click on the contact name, then click on the Tag button. To tag all contacts, click on the Tag All button.

- ✔ To scroll up (display earlier times) or down (display later times) in the day or week calendars, click the up or down scroll button.

- ✔ To scroll to another date, click the left and right scroll arrows beneath the view indicator(s).

✔ To change to a different view (day, week, or month), click the button that represents the desired view.

✔ To display a calendar, click the Calendar button (day or week view only).

✔ To print the calendar, click the Printer button. See the section "Printing a Calendar" for more information.

Moving from Contact to Contact

Using the day calendar is a good way to keep track of what you need to do on a particular day. Display the calendar. When you have the calendar on-screen, you can point to the call, meeting, or to-do item you need and double-click. ACT! displays the contact for that activity. When you clear the entry, ACT! asks if you are done with this contact. Choose Yes and ACT! displays the next scheduled contact.

Editing the Calendar Entries

With your schedule on-screen, you can make changes to any scheduled entries, schedule new entries, or clear entries. The following checklist summarizes your options:

✔ To reschedule an entry, click the entry in the calendar. Then choose the Schedule button. You see the Modify an Activity dialog box. Make the changes and choose OK.

✔ To schedule a new entry, click on the date and time you want to schedule the entry. Then choose the Schedule button. You see the Schedule an Activity dialog box. Enter the date, time, purpose, priority, type of activity, and other entries as described in Chapter 4. Remember that the scheduled activity is made for the current contact—that is, the contact that was on-screen when you displayed the calendar.

✔ To clear an activity, choose the Clear button and make an appropriate selection. Chapter 4 covers clearing calls, meetings, and to-do items in more detail.

✔ To group all contacts with scheduled activities, choose the Group button.

Printing a Calendar

To print the calendar, you need to setup your printer. Appendix A covers printer setup. You can choose to print a day, week, or month calendar. Follow these steps:

1. Choose the Report Print Calendar command.

   You see the ACT! Printouts dialog box (see fig. 5.13).

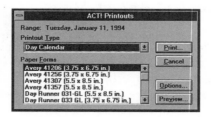

Figure 5.13. The ACT! Printouts dialog box.

2. Display the Printout Type drop-down list and select the type of calendar you want to print (Day, Week, or Month).

   By default, ACT! selects the type of calendar you last viewed.

3. In the Paper Forms list, select a paper type.

   You can purchase and use Day Runner paper in your printer. The Day Runner paper is similar to the type you use in a day planner. The options listed will vary depending on the type of calendar you select.

4. If you want to set print options, choose the Options button.

   You see the Calendar Options dialog box (see fig. 5.14).

Figure 5.14. The Calendar Options dialog box.

5. Check the activity items you want to print; uncheck items you don't want to print: Calls, Meetings, To-dos, Priority, and Public Activities.

6. From the Start Hour drop-down list, select the starting hour you want to use.

    The default is 8:00AM.

7. Check or uncheck any print options you want to change:

Option	Description
Company Name	Prints the company name
5 Week View	Prints a 5-week view of the calendar
Sat/Sun	Prints activities for Saturday and Sunday

8. If you want to enter a date range, choose the Date Range button. On the on-screen calendar that appears, drag across the date range you want to include, and then choose OK.

    You can print more than one day or month using this option.

TIP: *To preview information going into the printout, choose the Preview button. Make sure that the information is correct. Choose the Done button and then print the calendar.*

---

9. Choose OK.

    You are returned to the ACT! Printouts dialog box.

10. Choose Print.

    You see the Print dialog box (see fig. 5.15).

Figure 5.15. The Print dialog box.

11. Choose OK.

The address book is printed. Figures 5.16, 5.17, and 5.18 show a day, week, and month calendar printout, respectively.

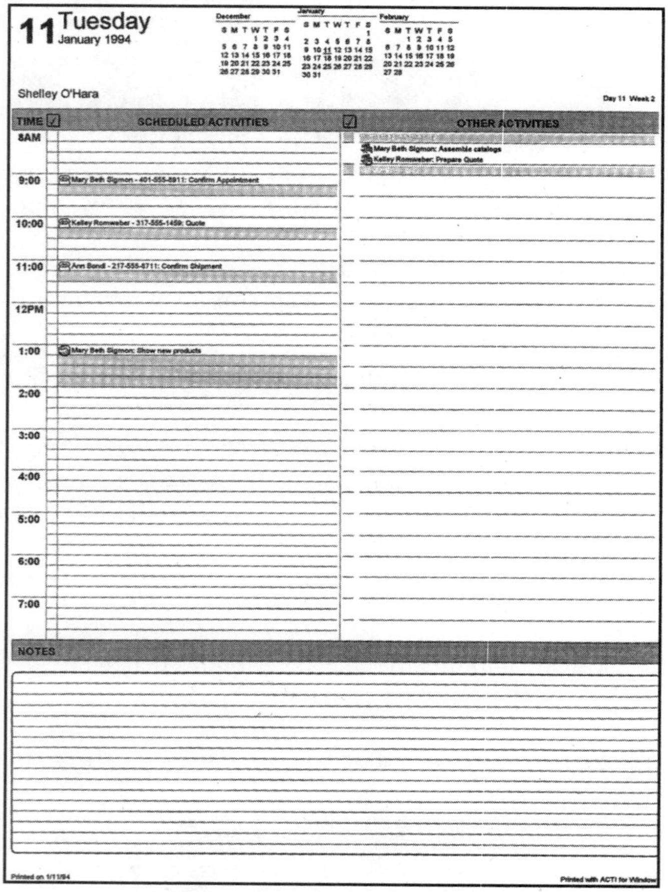

Figure 5.16. A day calendar printout.

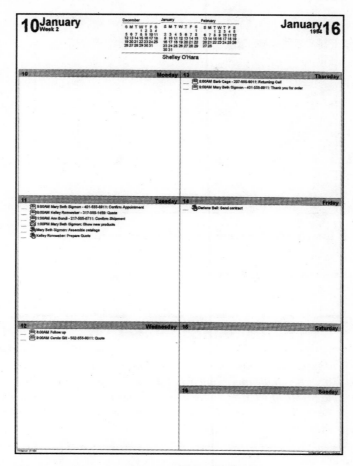

Figure 5.17. A week calendar printout.

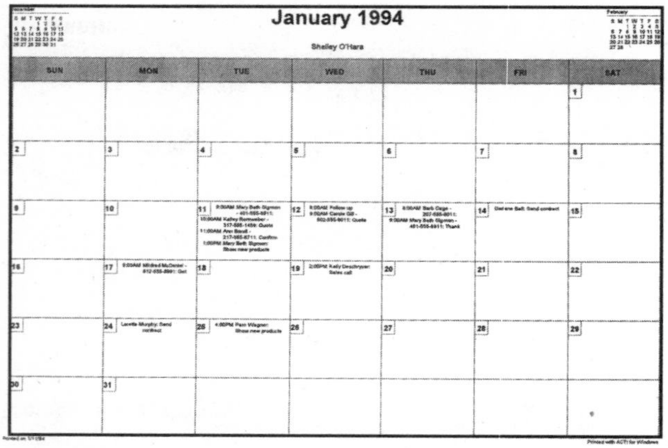

Figure 5.18. A month calendar printout.

For more information on printing reports, see Chapter 11.

Time-Management Tip

After you finish work for the day, organize your office or desk for the next day. Get rid of information you no longer need. Put information that you need to handle immediately in the center of your desk. Use visual reminders to highlight what you need to do. For instance, if you have a stack of mail to go through, put the mail right in the middle of your desk so that you have to face it.

TIP: *It's a good idea to back up your ACT! database periodically. For information on backing up, see Chapter 13, "Maintaining the Database."*

Q&A

How do I delete entries in the contact history?

✔ If you enter an activity using the wrong contact, you can delete the activity. In the history, click on the activity you want to delete. Then choose the Remove button. Choose Yes to remove the entry.

I can't print. What's the problem?

✔ To print, you must first setup your printer properly. Appendix A covers printer setup. For information on other print options, see Chapter 11.

What's the best way to track my activities?

ACT! provides many tools to schedule and manage your activities. Depending on your preferences and what you need to check, you may use a different tool. Consider these selections:

✔ When talking on the phone or when preparing a letter or report for a contact, review the contact history. This history will remind you of pertinent calls, meetings, and tasks. You can use this as you talk or write. For example, you can write "As we discussed on April 4..." All the details of all activities are listed.

✔ When you want an on-screen view of all the tasks you need to accomplish in a day, use the task list. The task list shows all calls, meetings, and to-do items. You can group the contacts easily so that you can make the calls, prepare for the meetings, and complete the to-dos.

✔ If you need a long range view of the week or month, use the View Week or View Month commands. These commands give you an overview of all your scheduled activities.

✔ If you prefer a printed copy of your schedule, use the Print Calendar command. This feature is useful if you plan to travel and don't have access to ACT! You also can use this feature to print and hand out calendars to remind other staff members or associates of key dates.

Using ACT! Mail

The world is indeed becoming a global village. With a modem and an on-line service, you can connect and send messages from one end of the country to the other in a few seconds. You can send messages from as far away as other countries to as close as the guy in the next office. If you are hooked to an e-mail system, you can use ACT! to create and send messages. You also can read messages that are sent to you. E-mail makes it quick and easy to respond to messages and send notes to other users. This chapter covers the following topics:

- Entering e-mail addresses
- Creating and sending messages
- Reading messages
- Using your Briefcase

CAUTION: *If you are not connected to an e-mail system, you cannot use the features described here. Also, keep in mind that you will need to know certain things about your e-mail system in order to set up and use this feature. If you have questions, consult your system adminstrator for the appropriate information.*

Time-Management Tip

Use time spent waiting and traveling. Plan this time to catch up on reading, or plan it as leisure time—daydreaming, reading a book, or doing crossword puzzles.

Entering E-Mail Addresses

ACT! needs to know information about the e-mail recipients—the kind of system and the user ID—and about your e-mail system. The second contact screen contains two e-mail fields: a field for the E-Mail System and a field for the E-Mail ID. You can enter the appropriate entries in the fields or you can use the menu to enter the mail system and ID. To use the menu, follow these steps:

1. Display the contact for whom you want to add e-mail addresses.

   You can scroll through the contacts or use a lookup to find the contact you want.

2. Choose the File Mail command.

   You see a submenu of choices.

3. Choose the E-mail Addresses.

   You see the E-mail Addresses dialog box (see fig. 6.1).

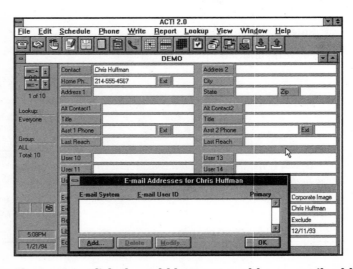

Figure 6.1. Click the Add button to add an e-mail address.

4. Choose the Add button.

   You see the Add E-Mail Address dialog box (see fig. 6.2).

5. From the E-mail System drop-down list, select the type of e-mail system.

   ACT! recognizes cc:Mail, CompuServe, and MS Mail. If this contact uses a different system, type it in the Other System text box.

6. Type the user ID in the E-mail User ID text box.

You need to ask the contact for his or her appropriate ID number.

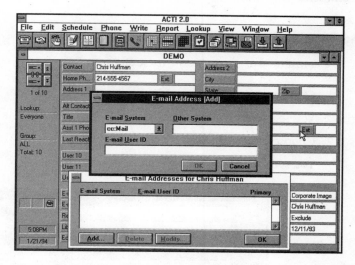

Figure 6.2. Select the E-mail System and enter the E-mail ID.

7. Choose OK.

The e-mail addresses are added to the contact screen. The following checklist summarizes other e-mail address tasks:

✔ If a user has more than one e-mail system, follow the same steps to enter the other e-mail systems and IDs. To select the primary e-mail address, click on it to mark it with a plus sign.

✔ To modify e-mail addresses, click the down arrow next to the appropriate contact field or choose the File Mail E-Mail Addresses command. Choose the Modify button and make changes, and then choose OK.

✔ To delete an e-mail address, choose the File Mail E-Mail Addresses command. Click the e-mail address that you want to delete. Then choose the Delete button. You are prompted to confirm the deletion. Choose Yes.

Creating and Sending a Message

After you enter the e-mail system and user ID, you can create and send messages. You can send the message to either one or several contacts. You can attach files—for example, other contacts or documents. You can send a message right after you create it, or you can put the message in your outbox and send the message later.

Creating Messages

To create a new message, follow these steps:

1. Choose the File Mail command.

   You see a submenu of choices.

2. Choose the Create Message command.

   You see the Create Message dialog box (see fig. 6.3).

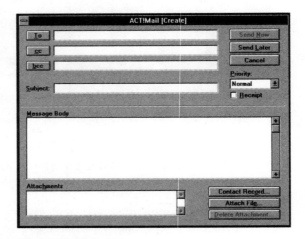

Figure 6.3. Creating a message.

3. Click the To button.

   You see a list of contact names (see fig. 6.4).

4. In the Address Book Entries, click on the contact to whom you want to send the message, and then click the Add button.

   The name is inserted in the To text box. You can send the message to additional contacts by clicking on the name and then clicking Add. To modify the e-mail information for a contact, click on the name and then click the Edit button. Make any changes and choose OK.

You also can send carbon copies or blind carbon copies by clicking the appropriate option button, clicking on names, and clicking the Add button.

By default, ACT! lists all ACT! Contacts. If you want to display only certain e-mail systems, select the system from the E-mail Systems drop-down list.

If you want to show only certain addresses, display the Address Book drop-down list and then select the addresses that you want displayed. For instance, you can display only America Online addresses.

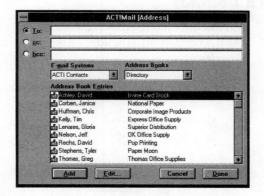

Figure 6.4. Selecting the To, cc, and bcc recipients.

5. After you finish creating the list of contacts, choose the Done button.

   You are returned to the Create dialog box.

6. Type the subject of the message in the Subject text box.

7. Display the Priority drop-down list and choose a priority.

   The choices are Normal, Low, or High.

8. If you want to receive confirmation that the e-mail is received, check the Receipt check box.

   By default, the message receipt is not acknowledged.

9. In the Message Body, type the text for the message.

If you want to attach a file (a contact record or other file), read the next section. If the message is ready to be sent, skip to the section, "Sending the Message."

Attaching a File

You can attach a group of contacts, an individual contact, or a file to the message. For example, you may want to pass on a lead to a colleague, so you attach the contact record. If you want to send a document—for example, a proposal—to a contact for her review, you can attach a file.

You can attach files when you create the message; the Create dialog box is displayed.

Attaching a Contact

You can attach one or several contact records to a message. You can attach just the contact information, or you can attach notes, activities, and histories.

To attach a contact record, follow these steps:

1. Choose the Contact Record button.

    You see the Select a Contact dialog box (see fig. 6.5).

Figure 6.5. The Select a Contact dialog box.

2. Select the contacts you want to include.

    To include a single contact, click on the contact. To include several contacts, click the first contact, then hold down the Ctrl key and click the next contacts until all contacts are selected. If the contact names are next to each other, you can click on the first name; then hold down the Shift key and click on the last one. All contacts between the first and last contacts are then selected. To attach all contacts in the current lookup group, choose the Attach Lookup button.

3. Check the type of information you want to include: Include Notes, Include History, and Include Activities.

By default, notes, histories, and activities are not included with the contact record.

4. Choose the OK button.

You are returned to the Create dialog box. The attachments are listed in the Attachments area. See the section "Sending the Message" for the next step.

Attaching a File

You can attach word processing files and other documents to a message. To attach a file, follow these steps:

1. Choose the Attach File button.

   You see the Choose File to Attach dialog box (see fig. 6.6).

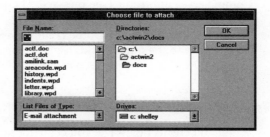

Figure 6.6. Choose the file you want to attach.

2. Click on the file name that you want to attach.

   If necessary, you can double-click on the directory in the Directories list to change directories.

3. Choose the OK button.

The attachment is listed in the Attachments text box. See the section "Sending the Message" to send the message and attached file.

Removing an Attachment

If you add an attachment by mistake, you can remove it. To remove an attachment, follow these steps:

1. In the Attachments area, click on the attachment you want to delete.

If no attachments are listed, you have not attached any files or contacts to the message. The Delete Attachment button is dimmed.

2. Choose the Delete Attachment button.

ACT! deletes the attachment from the message.

Sending the Message

After you create the message and attach any files or contacts, you are ready to send the message. You can send the message now or you can put the message in your outbox and send all the messages at once.

To send the message immediately, click the Send Now button. You'll probably see some initialization screens for your particular e-mail program. For instance, for CompuServe, ACT! initializes the modem, signs on to CompuServe, and readies the message. Then ACT! sends the message.

To put the message in the Outbox, click the Send Later button. ACT! adds the message to the outbox and displays a message telling you it has done so. Choose OK.

Opening Your Outbox

When you create a message, you can choose to send the message immediately or send it later. When you choose to send it later, the message is put in the outbox. You can review, edit, delete, or send messages in the outbox.

Follow these steps:

1. Choose the File Mail command.

   You see a submenu of choices.

2. Choose the Outbox command.

   You see the Outbox dialog box (see fig. 6.7). All the messages you have created, but not sent, are listed.

3. Take any of the following actions:

   To review a message, click on the message you want to read and then click the Read button in the icon bar. ACT! displays the message. You can make any changes and then choose Cancel to return to the outbox.

To print a message, click on the message you want to print. Then click the Print button. ACT! displays the Print dialog box. Choose OK to print the message.

To save a message, click on the message you want to save. Then click the Save button. ACT! displays the Save dialog box. Type a file name and choose OK.

To create a new message, click the New Message button. Create the new message, as described previously in this chapter.

To delete a message, click on the message and then click the Delete button. Confirm the deletion by choosing the Yes button.

To send a message, click on the message and then click the Send Now button. To send several messages, click on the first message. Hold down the Ctrl key and click on the next message you want to send. Do this until all the messages you want are selected. You also can click on the first message and then Shift+click on the last message to select all messages.

ACT! sends the message, informs you that it has been sent, and clears the outbox.

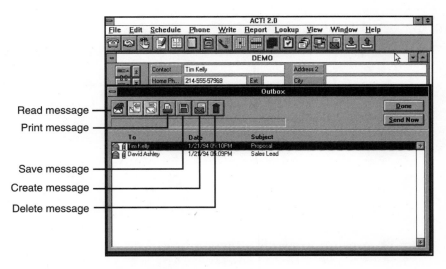

Figure 6.7. The Outbox.

Responding to Messages

Messages that you receive over e-mail are stored in your inbox. You can open your inbox and review, respond, print, delete, or forward the messages. Follow these steps:

1. Choose the File Mail command.

   You see a submenu.

2. Choose the Inbox command.

   If you are connected and logged onto an e-mail system, you see your Inbox (see fig. 6.8). All messages are listed. Red messages are high priority. A paper clip indicates the message has attachments.

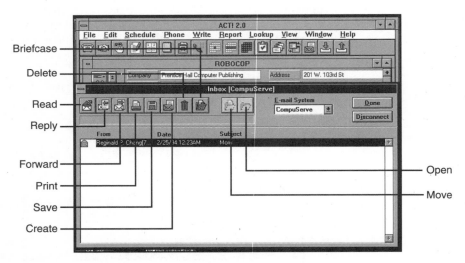

Figure 6.8. The Inbox.

> **NOTE:** *If you aren't logged onto an e-mail system, ACT! checks the My Record for appropriate information and logs on to the mail system specified. If you do not have an e-mail system identified, ACT! asks if you want to open your Briefcase. See the section, "Using Your Briefcase," for information.*

3. Click on the message you want and then click the Read button.

   ACT! displays the message on-screen (see fig. 6.9).

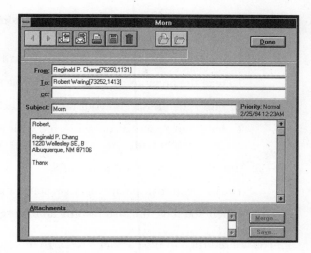

Figure 6.9. A message.

4. Take any of the following steps:

   To reply to the message, click the Reply button. You see the Reply/Forward Options dialog box (see fig. 6.10). Select which items you want to include and then click OK. ACT! displays the ACT! Mail dialog box (the same one you use to create a new message). Create and send the reply, as described previously in this chapter.

Figure 6.10. The Reply/Forward dialog box.

   To forward a message, click the Forward button. You see the Reply/Forward Options dialog box (see fig. 6.10). Select which items you want to include and click OK. Create and send the reply, as described earlier in this chapter.

   To print a message, click the Print button. ACT! displays the Print dialog box. Choose OK to print the message.

   To save a message, click the Save button. ACT! displays the Save dialog box. Type a file name and choose OK.

To delete a message, click the Delete button. Confirm the deletion by choosing the Yes button.

To read the next message, click the forward arrow.

To read the previous message, click the backward arrow.

To move the message to your briefcase, click the Briefcase button.

To merge an attached contact record with your database, click the contact attachment. Then click the Merge button.

5. Choose Done to return to the inbox.

   You also can manipulate messages from the inbox, as described in step 4.

6. When you have finished reading all messages, choose Done.

You are returned to the contact screen. To disconnect from the e-mail system, see the section, "Disconnecting."

Using Your Briefcase

If you want to respond to messages when you are not connected to the system, you can move the messages to your briefcase, as described in the preceding section. Later, you can open your briefcase and work with the messages.

To open your briefcase, follow these steps:

1. Disconnect from the e-mail system.

2. Choose the File Mail command.

   You see a submenu.

3. Choose the Inbox command.

   ACT! informs you that you are not logged on and asks whether you want to open your briefcase.

4. Choose Yes.

   You see your briefcase which contains all the messages you have placed there (see fig. 6.11).

5. Click on the message you want to work with, and then take any of the following actions:

   To read the message, click the Read button.

   To reply to the message, click the Reply button. You see the Reply/ Forward Options dialog box. Select which items you want to include and then click OK. Create the message. ACT! places the reply in the outbox. When you are connected to the e-mail system, send the reply from the outbox.

To forward a message, click the Forward button. You see the Reply/ Forward Options dialog box. Select which items you want to include and click OK. Create and send the reply, as described earlier in this chapter. ACT! places the reply in your outbox. When you are connected to the e-mail system, you need to forward the message from the outbox.

To print a message, click the Print button. ACT! displays the Print dialog box. Choose OK to print the message.

To save a message, click the Save button. ACT! displays the Save dialog box. Type a file name and choose OK.

To delete a message, click the Delete button. Confirm the deletion by choosing the Yes button.

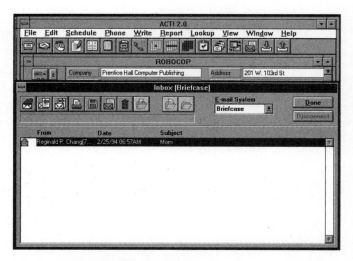

Figure 6.11. The Briefcase.

6. Choose Done.

You are returned to the contact screen.

Disconnecting

To disconnect from the e-mail system, choose the File Mail command. Then choose the Disconnect command. You are disconnected.

PART

Documents

Consulting Business Scenario

A consulting business is a combination of a sales and small business job. You may consider yourself a sales person because you sell your services, but you also may own your own business. Using ACT! you can help build your customer base and track key customer information, as shown in the following scenario:

As a consultant, it is important to remember *what* you promised to do *when*. Using ACT! you start the day by reviewing your calendar. The calendar displays the calls, meetings, and to-do items you need to complete for the day.

The first items for the day involve calls. Using the calendar, you move to the first contact and have ACT! dial the number. No one answers, so you make a note that you attempted the call and then reschedule the call for later. It's important to keep a history of the calls you attempted and completed.

The second call goes through. You have all the needed information right before you as you discuss a project. You turn on and use the timer (see Chapter 4, "Scheduling your Day") so that you can track the time spent. For some jobs, you bill by the hour.

The next item is a meeting with a consultant. You need to spend about one hour preparing for the meeting, so ACT! alerts you an hour before the meeting is scheduled. You spend the next hour putting together the proposal and price quote. You use the word processing program to create and polish the finished documents.

The meeting is a success; the client is interested in your services. You make a note on the contact screen and then schedule the follow-up activities—calls to make and so on.

You spend the last few minutes of the day reviewing your calendar. You clear all the items you completed and reschedule any items you didn't get to. You are confidently prepared for the next day.

This scenario gives some tips on using ACT! for a small business.

Contact Screen

In the consulting business, relationships with your clients are critical. You want to make sure that your clients feel as if you are up-to-date and fully informed about their business. You can use ACT! to track the information you need.

The contact screen in figure S3.1 was customized for a computer consultant. The consultant keeps track of the type of computer system, software used, and more.

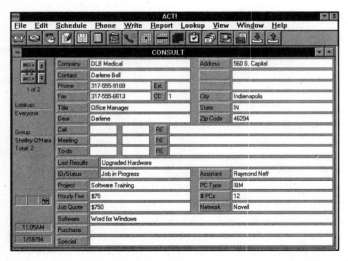

Figure S3.1. A contact screen designed for a computer consultant.

You may want to use the second contact screen to store personal information.

The popups for calls, meetings, and to-do items are sales oriented. You may want to modify the popups to contain entries pertinent to your business. Customizing the database is covered in Chapter 3, "Managing Contacts."

Reports

When you prepare an invoice for a client, you may want to print and review the contact history (see fig. S3.2). This history will remind you what you have accomplished for a particular client.

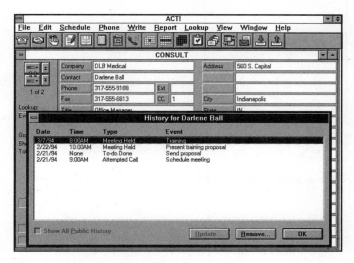

Figure S3.2. A contact history.

To keep track of the tasks for a day, use the task list. You can use the task list to display only top priority projects if you only have a certain amount of time.

Correspondence

In addition to standard documents such as letters, memos, and faxes, you can create proposals or quotes using ACT!'s word processing program. If you use the same format in your proposals, you can create and use a template. A template saves you the time of creating the same information over and over.

If you want to announce a new service, you can create a form letter to send to your clients (see fig. S3.3). You can merge the selected clients' names and addresses with the letter to create personalized letters.

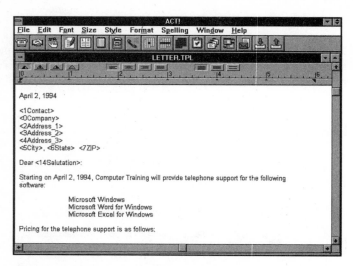

Figure S3.3. A form letter announcing a new service.

Creating Reports

When you work with the computer right in front of you, the on-screen displays are useful for reviewing contact information, your schedule, and other to-do items. If you are going to be away from the computer, however, you may want to make a printed copy of your schedule or other information. Or, you may prefer to print key information periodically so that you have a hard copy version.

With ACT!, you can use one of the several predefined report formats, or you can create your own report.

This chapter covers the following topics:

- Using a predefined report

- Creating a custom report

TIP: *For information on creating labels, see Chapter 11.*

Using a Predefined Report

ACT! is a well-designed program, which means that the programmers put a great deal of thought into how you are going to use the program and which information is most important to you. The programmers set up several predefined report formats useful for many different purposes, and if one of the predefined formats doesn't suit your needs, you can create your own report, as described in the following section.

Reviewing the Available Reports

The predefined reports set up in ACT! follow:

✔ **Print Calendar:** Prints a daily, weekly, or monthly version of your calendar. Chapter 5 covers printing this report.

✔ **Print Address Book:** Prints a list of all contacts and key contact information. Chapter 3 covers this report.

✔ **Activities Completed:** Prints a list of all completed activities. You can choose the dates and contacts included in the report. Figure 7.1 shows this type of report.

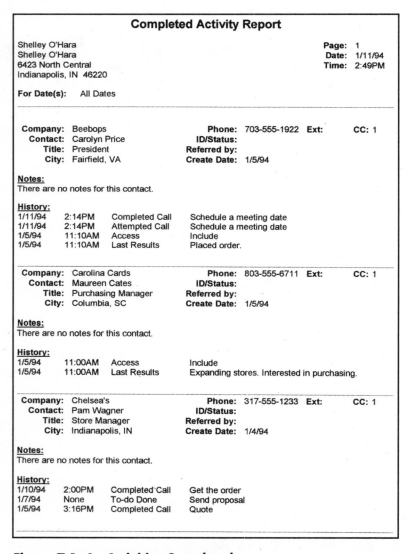

Figure 7.1. An Activities Completed report.

✔ **History Summary:** Prints a summary of a contacts history (attempted calls, completed calls, meetings held, and letters sent). You can choose the dates and contacts included in the report. Figure 7.2 shows this type of report.

History Summary Report

Shelley O'Hara
Shelley O'Hara
6423 North Central

Indianapolis, IN 46220

Page: 1
Report Date: 1/11/94
Time: 2:52PM
Contacts: 12

For Date(s):   All Dates

Contact	Attempted Calls	Completed Calls	Meetings Held	Letters Sent
Carolyn Price	1	1	0	0
Maureen Cates	0	0	0	0
Pam Wagner	0	2	0	0
Darlene Ball	0	2	0	0
Carole Gill	0	0	0	0
Loretta Murphy	0	0	0	0
Mary Beth Sigmon	0	0	1	0
Mildred McDaniel	0	0	0	0
Kelley Romweber	2	2	0	0
Kelly Deschryver	0	0	1	0
Ann Bondi	0	0	0	0
Barb Cage	0	0	0	0
Totals:	**3**	**7**	**2**	**0**

Figure 7.2. History Summary report.

✔ **Future Activity:** Prints a list of all future activities (see fig. 7.3).

✔ **Task List:** Prints a task list (calls, meetings, and to-do items). You can choose the dates and contacts included in the report. A task list is shown in figure 7.4.

Future Activity Report

Shelley O'Hara
Shelley O'Hara
6423 North Central

Indianapolis, IN 46220

Page:	1
Report Date:	1/11/94
Time:	2:52PM
Number of Profiles:	12

Company	Contact	Phone	Ext	CC
Beebops	Carolyn Price	703-555-1922		1

Type	Date	Time	Regarding
There are no activities for this contact.			

Company	Contact	Phone	Ext	CC
Carolina Cards	Maureen Cates	803-555-6711		1

Type	Date	Time	Regarding
Meeting	2/28/94	8:00AM	Sales call

Company	Contact	Phone	Ext	CC
Chelsea's	Pam Wagner	317-555-1233		1

Type	Date	Time	Regarding
Meeting	1/25/94	4:00PM	Show new products
To-do	2/14/94	None	Send FAX

Company	Contact	Phone	Ext	CC
Darlene's Gagdets	Darlene Ball	317-255-9731		1

Type	Date	Time	Regarding
To-do	1/14/94	None	Send contract

Company	Contact	Phone	Ext	CC
Fun City	Carole Gill	502-555-9011		1

Type	Date	Time	Regarding
Call	1/12/94	9:00AM	Quote
Call	2/16/94	9:00AM	Follow up

Figure 7.3. Future Activity report.

Task List Report

Shelley O'Hara
Shelley O'Hara
6423 North Central
Indianapolis, IN 46220

Page: 1
Date: 1/11/94
Time: 2:53PM

For Date(s): 1/10/94 - 1/14/94

Calls:

Company	Contact	Phone	Ext	CC	Date	Time
Mary's	Mary Beth Sigmon	401-555-8911		1	1/11/94	9:00AM
Rockys	Kelley Romweber	317-555-1459		1	1/11/94	10:00AM
Surprise!	Ann Bondi	217-555-8711		1	1/11/94	11:00AM
Shelley O'Hara	Shelley O'Hara	317-555-5510		1	1/12/94	8:00AM
Fun City	Carole Gill	502-555-9011		1	1/12/94	9:00AM
The Perfect Gift	Barb Cage	207-555-9011		1	1/13/94	8:00AM
Mary's	Mary Beth Sigmon	401-555-8911		1	1/13/94	9:00AM

Total Calls: 7

Meetings:

Company	Contact	Phone	Ext	CC	Date	Time
There are no Meetings scheduled in this date range.						

Total Meetings: 0

To-dos:

Company	Contact	Date	Regarding
Mary's	Mary Beth Sigmon	1/11/94	Assemble catalogs
Rockys	Kelley Romweber	1/11/94	Prepare Quote
Darlene's Gagdets	Darlene Ball	1/14/94	Send contract

Total To-dos: 3

Figure 7.4. A task list.

✔ **Status Report:** Prints the company, contact, phone, address,
ID/Status, and Last Results for the contacts (see fig. 7.5).

```
                        Status Report

Shelley O'Hara                                   Page:  1
Shelley O'Hara                           Report Date:  1/11/94
6423 North Central                              Time:  2:53PM
Indianapolis, IN 46220

For Dates:    All Dates                 Number of Profiles:  12
```

Company Contact Phone	Ext	CC	ID/Status Last Results RE	Date
Beebops Carolyn Price 703-555-1922		1	Placed order.	
Carolina Cards Maureen Cates 803-555-6711		1	Expanding stores. Interested in purchasing.	
Chelsea's Pam Wagner 317-555-1233		1	Send FAX	2/14/94
Darlene's Gagdets Darlene Ball 317-255-9731		1	Send contract	1/14/94
Fun City Carole Gill 502-555-9011		1	Order Pending	
House of Cards Loretta Murphy 201-555-4312		1	Sale pending. Send contract	1/24/94
Mary's Mary Beth Sigmon 401-555-8911		1	Assemble catalogs	1/11/94
Millie's Mildred McDaniel 812-555-8991		1	Order Pending.	

Figure 7.5. A status report.

✔ **Contact Report:** Prints all contact fields, history, notes, and activities for the contacts you choose, as shown in figure 7.6.

```
                        Contact Report

Shelley O'Hara                                    Page:  1
Shelley O'Hara                                    Date:  1/11/94
6423 North Central                                Time:  2:54PM
Indianapolis, IN  46220               Number of Contacts:  12


   Company:  Beebops                   Address:  6708 George Ave.
   Contact:  Carolyn Price
     Phone:  703-555-1922   Ext:        CC:  1
     Title:  President                    City:  Fairfield
 Assistant:                              State:  VA
      Dear:  Carolyn                  Zip Code:  22020

      Call:                            RE:
   Meeting:                            RE:
     To-do:                            RE:

 Last Results:   Placed order.
     ID/Status:                       Referred by:

 # of Stores:  3                    Assist. Phone:
  Store Size:  Medium                    User 5:
  Store Type:  Cards, Gifts, Balloons, Gag Gifts     User 6:

     User 7:
     User 8:
     User 9:

   Contact:  Carolyn Price               City:
Home Phone:                  Ext:        State:
 Address 1:                               Zip:

Alt Contact1:                       Alt Contact2:
      Title:                              Title:
Asst 1 Phone:                Ext:    Asst 2 Phone:           Asst 2 Phone:
 Last Reach:                          Last Reach:

    User 10:                             User 13:
    User 11:                             User 14:
    User 12:                             User 15:

History:
1/11/94      2:14PM      Completed Call     Schedule a meeting date
1/11/94      2:14PM      Attempted Call     Schedule a meeting date
1/5/94       11:10AM     Access             Include
1/5/94       11:10AM     Last Results       Placed order.


Notes:
There are no notes for this contact.

Activities:
There are no activities for this contact.
```

Figure 7.6. A contact report.

✔ **Notes:** Prints the notes for all selected contacts. Figure 7.7 shows a Notes report.

```
                    Notes Report by Profile

Shelley O'Hara                               Page:  1
Shelley O'Hara                               Date:  1/11/94
6423 North Central                           Time:  2:59PM
Indianapolis, IN 46220

For Date(s):  All Dates                      Contacts:  3
─────────────────────────────────────────────────────────────

   Company: Fun City              Phone:  502-555-9011 Ext:   CC:
   Contact: Carole Gill           ID/Status:
     Title: Regional Manager      Referred by:  Kathleen Marbaugh
      City: Louisville, KY        Create Date:  1/5/94

Notes:
Recently promoted to Regional Manager. Has been with company 12 years. Knows product very
           well.

Interested in expanding market. Busy for next few months, but would like to set up sales demo in
           March.



─────────────────────────────────────────────────────────────
   Company: House of Cards        Phone:  201-555-4312 Ext:   CC:
   Contact: Loretta Murphy        ID/Status:
     Title: Sales Manager         Referred by:  Carolyn Price
      City: Philadelphia, PA      Create Date:  1/5/94

Notes:
Willing to experiment. Has very large inventory and likes to try new products.

Very interested in art products.



─────────────────────────────────────────────────────────────
   Company: The Perfect Gift      Phone:  207-555-9011 Ext:   CC:
   Contact: Barb Cage             ID/Status:
     Title: Sales Manager         Referred by:
      City: Williamsburg, VA      Create Date:  1/5/94

Notes:
Stocks mostly gift items. Is willing to look at art products.

─────────────────────────────────────────────────────────────
```

Figure 7.7 A Notes report.

✔ **Directory:** Prints the primary and secondary address and phone numbers for the selected contacts (see fig. 7.8).

Directory

Shelley O'Hara
Shelley O'Hara
6423 North Central
Indianapolis, IN 46220

Page: 1
Report Date: 1/11/94
Time: 2:58PM
Number of Contacts: 12

Primary

Secondary

Beebops
Carolyn Price
703-555-1922   Ext: CC: Sec: President
6708 George Ave.

Fairfield
VA
22020

Carolina Cards
Maureen Cates
803-555-6711   Ext: CC: Sec: Purchasing Manager
6708 Little O Street   803-555-8911
                                        709 Green Street

Columbia   Columbia
SC   SC
29212   29227

Chelsea's
Pam Wagner
317-555-1233   Ext: CC: Sec: Store Manager
6501 Guilford   317-555-5777

Indianapolis
IN
46220

Darlene's Gagdets
Darlene Ball
317-255-9731   Ext: CC: Sec: President

IN
46220

Fun City
Carole Gill
502-555-9011   Ext: CC: Sec: Regional Manager
6709 Derby Lane   502-555-4311
                                        7809 South River Street

Louisville   Lousiville
KY   KY
40207   40207

Figure 7.8. A Directory report.

✔ **Phone:** Prints the phone number for selected contacts (see fig. 7.9).

Phone List

Shelley O'Hara	**Page:**	1
Shelley O'Hara	**Report Date:**	1/11/94
6423 North Central	**Time:**	2:59PM
Indianapolis, IN 46220	**Number of Contacts:**	12

<u>Company</u>	<u>Contact</u>	<u>Phone</u>	<u>Ext</u>	<u>CC</u>
Beebops	Carolyn Price	703-555-1922		1
Carolina Cards	Maureen Cates	803-555-6711		1
Chelsea's	Pam Wagner	317-555-1233		1
Darlene's Gagdets	Darlene Ball	317-255-9731		1
Fun City	Carole Gill	502-555-9011		1
House of Cards	Loretta Murphy	201-555-4312		1
Mary's	Mary Beth Sigmon	401-555-8911		1
Millie's	Mildred McDaniel	812-555-8991		1
Rockys	Kelley Romweber	317-555-1459		1
Special Gifts	Kelly Deschryver	317-555-0118		1
Surprise!	Ann Bondi	217-555-8711		1
The Perfect Gift	Barb Cage	207-555-9011		1

Figure 7.9. A phone list.

Creating the Report

You follow the same basic steps when printing a report. Some options vary, depending on the type of report you select.

> **TIP:** *If you want to include only certain contacts in the report, first create a lookup group. See Chapter 3 for more information on lookup groups.*

Follow these basic steps:

1. Open the Report menu.

   You see a list of predefined reports.

2. Choose the report you want.

   Depending on the kind of report you choose, you see either an on-screen calendar (see fig. 7.10) or the Prepare Report dialog box. If you see the calendar, follow the next step. Otherwise, skip to step 4.

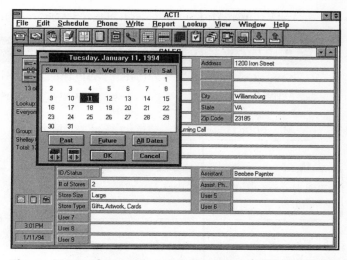

Figure 7.10. The on-screen calendar enables you to select the dates you want to include in the report.

3. To tell ACT! which dates to include, take one of the following actions:

To include all past dates, choose the Past button.

To include all future dates, choose the Future button.

To include all dates, choose the All Dates button.

To include a range of dates, click and hold down the mouse button on the first date. Then drag across the dates you want to include. Choose OK.

The calendar appears for these reports: Activities Completed, History Summary, Task List, and Notes.

You see the Prepare Report dialog box (see fig. 7.11).

Figure 7.11. The Prepare Report dialog box.

4. In the Use area, choose which contacts to include:

Option	Description
Active Contact	Includes only the active contact.
Active Lookup	Includes all contacts in the active lookup.
All Contacts	Includes all contacts.

TIP: *When you choose the Task List, the only option available is All Contacts.*

---

5. Choose OK.

   By default, the report is displayed on-screen. You can send the report directly to the printer by choosing Printer in the Output area. Then choose OK.

   You see the report on-screen. Displaying the report on-screen enables you to check that the report is what you intended. You may have selected the wrong report type or included the wrong dates.

6. To print the report, choose the File Print command.

   You see the Print dialog box.

7. Choose OK.

The report is printed. For information on setting up your printer, see Appendix A.

If you want to save the file, choose the File Save command and type a file name in the text box. The file is saved as a word processing (WPD) file. To close the report, double-click the Control menu box. If you haven't saved the report, you are prompted to save changes. Choose Yes to save the file or No to close the file without saving the changes.

Creating a Custom Report

If none of the reports are just what you need, you can create and use a custom report. If you plan to use this report fairly often, you can have ACT! add the custom report to the Report menu.

The custom report is called a *template*. You also can create word processing templates, as described in Chapter 9.

Viewing an Existing Report

To understand how to set up a report, you may want to take a look at an existing report template to see the types of fields that are inserted and the way the report is formatted.

To view an existing report template, follow these steps:

1. Choose the File Open command.

2. Display the List Files of Type drop-down list and select Report Template.

   You see a list of report templates.

3. Click on a report template you want to view.

4. Click on OK.

Figure 7.12 shows the Directory template. Notice how the report is put together. The name of the report is typed in manually. The information about the company is inserted from "My Record." The lines are added manually. The field labels and field contents for the address and phone fields are inserted between the lines. The <Start Contact> and <End Contact> fields tell ACT! to pull the information from all contacts.

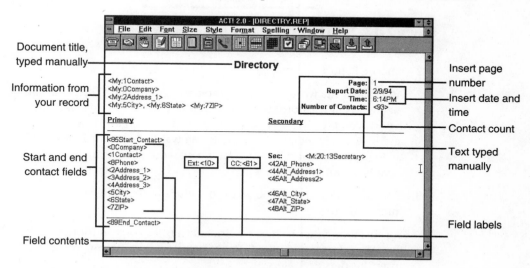

Figure 7.12. A predefined report template.

To close the template, choose the File Close command.

Creating a New Report Template

Setting up a new template can take time. You need to know what you want to include and the order in which you want the information included. Looking at a predefined template should give you an idea of what you need to include.

> **TIP:** *First, sketch out the report on paper so that you have a plan as you create the template.*

To create a new report template, follow these steps:

1. Choose the File New command.

   You see the New File dialog box (see fig. 7.13).

Figure 7.13. The New File dialog box.

2. Choose Report Template.

   ACT! starts the word processing program and displays the Field Names dialog box at the bottom of the screen (see fig. 7.13). To create the report, you type the text you want included (such as the report name) and insert the field and field labels you want to compile by using the dialog box. For more information on all word processing features, see Chapters 8 and 9.

3. Type any information you want to include as unchangeable information.

   For instance, you may want to include a title. You can format the title to make it larger and in a different typeface, if you want. You can also insert headers or footers.

   You may also want to include information about your company to identify to whom the report belongs. You then include specific field labels and field data from your contacts, as described in the next step.

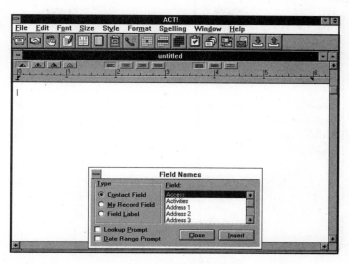

Figure 7.14. Creating a report template.

3. To insert a field or field label, take one of the actions listed in the following checklist:

   ✔ To insert a range of contacts, insert the <Start Contact> field, then insert the contact information you want to include, and finally insert the <End Contact> Field.

   ✔ To add a field label from the contact screen, choose the Field Label option. In the Field list, click on the field you want to insert. Then click Insert. Keep in mind that this inserts the *label*, not the data from the field.

   ✔ To insert data from a particular field, choose the Contact Field option. In the Field list, click on the field you want to insert. Then click the Insert button. When you use this option, ACT! collects and prints data from that field in the report.

   ✔ To insert data from your own record, choose the My Record option. In the Field list, click on the field you want to insert. Then click the Insert button. In the top part of the report, you may want to include your company name and your name. Use the My Record option to do this.

4. Continue adding fields until the report is complete.

   You can include as many fields as you want. Figure 7.15 shows a custom report that includes the contact name and fax number for all contacts.

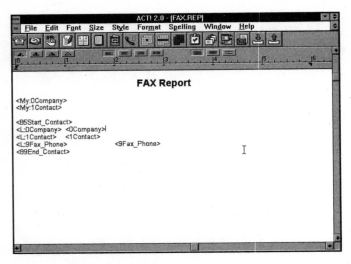

Figure 7.15. A custom report.

5. If you want ACT! to prompt you for a date range when you run the report, check the Date Range Prompt check box. If you want to prompt for which group to include, check the Lookup Prompt check box.

    These prompts appear if the box is checked and do not appear if the box is not checked.

6. After you finish creating the report, choose the File Save command to save the file.

    You see the Save dialog box. By default, all templates are saved in the C:\ACTWIN2\REPORTS directory and use the extension REP.

7. In the File Name text box, type a file name and choose OK.

The report is saved. To use the report, see the section, "Using the Custom Report."

Tips on Creating Reports

Creating a custom report isn't an easy task. You have to spend some time working in the report template, running the report, noting all problems, and then editing the template again. Consider the following tips:

✔ *You may have to tinker with the alignment of the fields and field labels. The report template may appear as if the information is*

> aligned properly, but when you run the report, entries may not align
> as expected.
>
> ✔ You can use the word processing formatting features—such as bold,
> font changes, headers and footers—to create a more polished report.
> See Chapter 9, "Formatting Documents."
>
> ✔ Use the information in the record to add your company name and
> company information to the top of the report.
>
> ✔ Consider adding a big, bold, centered title at the top to indicate the
> name of the report.

Editing the Report Template

If you need to edit the report template—for example, add more information
or rearrange the organization—you can do so.

> **CAUTION:** *Although you can, it's not a good idea to edit the predefined
> report templates. If you corrupt the template, you cannot then run the
> predefined report.*

To edit the report template, follow these steps:

1. Choose the Report Edit Template command.

   You see the Select Report dialog box. It lists all available report
   templates.

2. Double-click on the template you want to change, or click once on the
   template name and then click OK.

   ACT! displays the template on-screen.

3. Make any changes and then use the File Save command to save the
   template.

For more information on the available word processing features, see
Chapters 8 and 9, "Using the Word Processor" and "Formatting
Documents."

Using the Custom Report Template

The report templates provided with ACT! are the reports you can create
from the menu. You can also create labels.

When you want to use the custom report that you created, follow these steps:

1. Choose the Report Other command.

   You see the Select Report dialog box (see fig. 7.16).

Figure 7.16. Select the report you want to use.

2. Double-click on the template name.

   If you checked the Date Range Prompt you see the on-screen calendar.

3. Select a date range, if necessary.

   You see the Prepare Report dialog box.

4. Choose OK to display the report on-screen.

After the report is on-screen, you can choose to save the file (File Save) or print the file (File Print). Figure 7.17 shows the FAX report.

Adding the Template to the Menu

If you use the report often, you may want to add it to the menu. First, create and save the report as described in the previous sections. Then follow these steps:

1. Choose the Report Modify Menu command.

   You see the Custom Report dialog box (see fig. 7.18).

FAX Numbers

Works of Art
Shelley O'Hara

Company	Beebops
Contact	Carolyn Price
Fax	703-555-5451
Company	Carolina Cards
Contact	Maureen Cates
Fax	803-555-6188
Company	Chelsea's
Contact	Pam Wagner
Fax	317-555-9056
Company	Darlene's Gagdets
Contact	Darlene Ball
Fax	317-555-1209
Company	Fun City
Contact	Carole Gill
Fax	502-555-6099
Company	House of Cards
Contact	Loretta Murphy
Fax	201-555-7001
Company	Mary's
Contact	Mary Beth Sigmon
Fax	401-555-7123
Company	Millie's
Contact	Mildred McDaniel
Fax	812-555-6122
Company	Rockys
Contact	Kelley Romweber
Fax	317-555-2388
Company	Special Gifts
Contact	Kelly Deschryver
Fax	371-555-6411
Company	Surprise!
Contact	Ann Bondi
Fax	217-555-9111
Company	The Perfect Gift
Contact	Barb Cage
Fax	207-555-4788

Figure 7.17. The FAX report.

Figure 7.18. The Custom Report dialog box.

2. Choose the Add button.

You see the Add Custom Menu Item dialog box (see fig. 7.19).

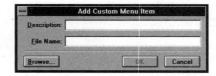

Figure 7.19. The Add Custom Menu Item dialog box.

3. In the Description text box, type the name you want to have appear on the menu.

For example, you might type FAX for a report that lists only FAX numbers.

4. In the File Name text box, type the name of the report template.

Type the same name you used when you saved the report template. Be sure to type the extension, too.

> **TIP:** *If you can't remember the name, click the Browse button. By default, ACT! stores all queries in the directory C:\ACTWIN2\REPORTS. You see the files in this directory. Double-click on the file name.*

5. Choose OK.

You are returned to the Custom Report dialog box. The new menu item is listed in the dialog box.

6. Choose OK.

You are returned to the contact screen.

The following checklist summarizes how to execute, rearrange, and delete a custom report from the menu:

✔ To execute the custom report, choose the Report command. You should see the report name listed at the bottom of the menu. Click on the name to select and execute the report.

✔ To delete an item from the menu, choose the Report Modify Menu command. Click on the menu item you want to delete. Then click the Delete button. Keep in mind that this process deletes the menu item but does not delete the report file stored on disk.

✔ To rearrange several menu items, choose the Report Modify Menu command. Click the menu item that you want to change, and then click Item Up or Item Down.

✔ To separate queries by lines, choose the Report Modify Menu command. Click the Add Line button. A line is added above the current item. (You can adjust the placement of the line by clicking on it and clicking the Item Up or Item Down button.

Q&A

My printer won't print.

✔ For your printer to work properly, it must be hooked up and installed. See Appendix A for more information on setting up the printer.

My report only includes entries for one contact. What's wrong?

✔ For most reports, you can choose to include the current contact, the contacts in the current lookup, or all contacts. Rerun the report and be sure that you have not selected current contact. If this option is selected, the report will include only the current contact. This time choose Active Lookup or All Contacts.

Why doesn't my report include the entries I expected?

✔ If your report is missing calls, meetings, or to-do items, be sure that you used a correct date range. If you want past dates, click the Past button. If you want future dates, click the Future button. If you want a date range, drag across the range you want. If you select a date range, double-check that you have included the proper date range.

✔ If the report is missing contacts, make sure that you are using the right Active Lookup. To include all contacts, choose the All Contacts option button.

My report includes too many contacts. Can I change it?

✔ Your contact database can include hundreds of entries. Usually, you won't want to include every contact. To control which contacts are included, create a lookup group as described in Chapter 3. Then choose Active Lookup when you run the report.

Using the Word Processor

As you do business, you probably are not just limited to phone calls and meetings as the only form of communication. You may need to create a proposal for a client or send a letter. You may need to type a quote or some other document. ACT! includes a built-in word processor that you can use to create documents.

NOTE: *ACT! sets up different document templates for memos, faxes, and letters. These features are covered in Chapter 10, "Creating Letters, Memos, and Faxes." The basics of typing, saving, and editing these kinds of documents are the same. See this chapter for information on typing and editing. Skim Chapter 9, "Formatting Documents," for information about formatting, and then use the information in Chapter 10 to create the letter, memo, or fax.*

This chapter covers the following topics:

- Creating a document
- Typing text
- Editing text
- Saving and opening documents
- Inserting the date and time
- Searching and replacing text
- Checking your spelling

Creating a Document

Usually in ACT!, you work in the contact screens—scheduling calls, entering contact information, setting up meetings, tracking your schedule. This is why you see the database contact screen whenever you start ACT!.

When you want to create another kind of document, you need to open a document window. To create a word processing document, follow these steps:

1. Choose the File New command.

   You see the New File dialog box. Notice the types of documents you can create.

2. Choose the Document button.

   ACT! starts the word processing program and displays a blank word processing document on-screen (see fig. 8.1). Take some time to identify the key on-screen elements.

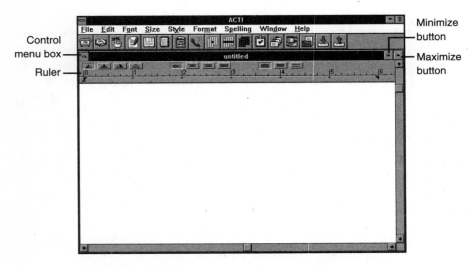

Figure 8.1. A blank word processing document.

The Control menu box, Maximize button, and Minimize button help you control the size of the window. Chapter 1, "Getting Started," covers working with windows in more detail. The Ruler is helpful for document formatting, covered in Chapter 9.

You can hide the Ruler by choosing the Format Hide Ruler command. To display page guides, choose the Format Show Page Guides command.

Time Management Tip

Some tasks, such as writing, always take more time than you expect. Plan extra time for these kinds of activities.

Typing Text

Type text by using the alphanumeric keys on the keyboard. Type just as you type on a typewriter. Notice that a flashing vertical line, called the *insertion point*, moves as you type. This insertion point indicates where the next character you type appears. You can move the insertion point around on-screen, as described in the following section.

When you type on a typewriter, you need to manually insert carriage returns when you reach the end of the line. With a word processing program, however, you don't have to worry about line breaks. Just keep typing. When a word doesn't fit on a line, ACT! moves the word to the next line. The following checklist summarizes the key points you need to keep in mind when typing:

✔ Press Enter when you want to end a paragraph and start the next one. Don't press Enter to end each line.

✔ To insert a tab, press the Tab key. ACT! moves the insertion point over the default tab distance. (For more information on setting tabs, see Chapter 4, "Scheduling Your Day.")

✔ ACT! also inserts page breaks as needed. If you need to force a page break—for instance, suppose that you have a title page with the title, date, and company name—press Shift+Enter. You can also choose the Format Insert Page Break command to insert a page break.

✔ If you make a mistake and want to delete the character you just typed, press Backspace. Pressing Backspace deletes characters to the left of the insertion point. Pressing Delete deletes characters to the right of the insertion point.

Time-Management Tip

Plan time for fun and relaxation.

Moving Around

The insertion point, as mentioned, is similar to the You Are Here arrow. It shows you where text you type is inserted. When you want to make a change to text you've already typed, you first move the insertion point to the spot. Then you can make the change—delete or add text.

You can use the mouse or the keyboard to move around on-screen. To use the mouse, use the mouse pointer to point to where you want to insert the insertion point. Then click the mouse button. The insertion point moves to the point you clicked.

To use the keyboard, use any of the keystrokes listed in table 8.1.

Table 8.1. Moving Around Using the Keyboard

Press	To move
→	One character right
←	One character left
↑	One line up
↓	One line down
Home	Beginning of the line
End	End of the line
PgUp	Previous screen
PgDn	Next screen
Ctrl+Home	Top of the document
Ctrl+End	End of the document
Ctrl+PgUp	Top of screen
Ctrl+PgDn	Bottom of screen

Editing Text

When you type on a typewriter, the words are committed to paper. Making a change means using a product such as Liquid Paper and retyping over text. If the changes are substantial, you may need to retype the entire document again. With a word processing program, it is easy to add, delete, move, and copy text.

Adding Text

To add text, just move the insertion point where you want the new text to appear and type. ACT! moves existing text to the right to make room for the new text.

TIP: *If you want to replace existing text with new text, select the text first (described in the next section). Then type the new text. ACT! deletes the selected text and inserts the new text.*

Time Management Tip

Jot down ideas as they occur to you. Keep a notebook with you at all times.

Selecting Text

For most editing and formatting tasks, you need to first select the text you want to work with. Selecting text highlights the text you want to change— move, delete, copy, make bold, and so on.

You can select text using the mouse or the keyboard. To use the mouse, click at the start of the text you want to select. Hold down the mouse button and drag across the text you want to select. Then release the mouse button. The text appears in reverse video on-screen (see fig. 8.2).

To select text with the keyboard, move the insertion point to the start of the text you want to select. Press and hold down the Shift key and use the cursor movement keys—any of the arrow keys, Home, End, and so on—to select text. Table 8.1 lists the cursor movement keys.

To select the entire document, choose the Edit Select All command or press Ctrl+A.

To deselect text, click outside the selected text or release the Shift key and press any other key.

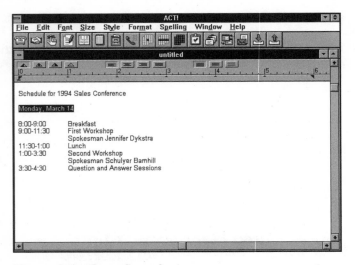

Figure 8.2. The selected text.

> **TIP:** *Double-click the mouse button quickly to select a word. To select a large passage of text, click at the start of the passage. Move to the end of the passage. Then press and hold down the Shift key and click the mouse button. All text between the two points is selected.*

Deleting Text

Deleting a character or two at a time is easy with the Backspace and Delete keys. When you want to delete a great deal of text, using these keys isn't the best method. Instead, select the text you want to delete. Then press the Delete key. ACT! deletes the selected text and moves up and over existing text to fill in the gap.

> **TIP:** *If you delete text by accident, don't panic. All you need to do is choose the Edit Undo command, and the text will be restored. If, however, you take some other action before choosing Edit Undo, the text is lost. Undo works on the last action performed, and if you do something else after you delete, you won't be able to undo the deletion.*

Moving Text

One benefit of using a word processing program is that you don't need to worry about getting the content of the document right the first time. Using a word processing program, you can compose the text easily as the ideas come to you and then go back and edit the text to make it flow. For example, after you compose the document, you may find that an idea you mentioned in the closing belongs in the opening. You can move this text easily.

To move text, follow these steps:

1. Select the text that you want to move.

   Selecting text is covered in the preceding section. You can select as much or as little text as you want.

2. Choose the Edit Cut command.

TIP: *To choose the Edit Cut command, press Ctrl+X.*

The text is cut from the document and stored in a temporary holding spot in memory known as the Clipboard. The Clipboard can store only one piece of information at a time. If you cut something else, the new data overwrites the first text you selected.

3. Move to the point where you want to place the cut text.

   You can use either the mouse or the keyboard to move to the new location.

4. Choose the Edit Paste command.

TIP: *To choose the Edit Paste command, press Ctrl+P.*

Copying Text

If you need to repeat information in a document, you can copy it. Copying text is useful to repeat the same information, but in a slightly different way. You can copy and edit the second version so that you convey the same idea.

To copy text, follow these steps:

1. Select the text that you want to copy.

   Figure 8.3 shows the selected text to be copied.

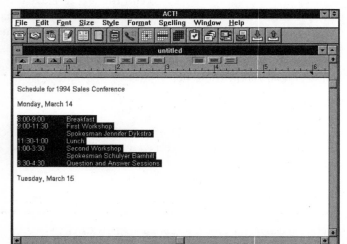

Figure 8.3. The selected text, about to be copied.

2. Choose the Edit Copy command.

   The text is copied to the Clipboard and remains in the document.

TIP: *Press Ctrl+C to choose the Edit Copy command.*

---

3. Move the insertion point to where you want to place the copy.

   You can use the keyboard or the mouse to move the insertion point.

4. Choose the Edit Paste command.

The copied text is pasted in the new location (see fig. 8.4).

TIP: *Press Ctrl+P to choose the Edit Paste command. Also, to paste text more than once, move to the new location and choose Edit Paste. ACT! pastes the same information again. The Clipboard stores the copied text until you copy or cut additional text.*

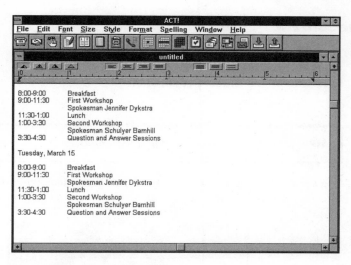

Figure 8.4. The copied text.

To undo the copy, choose the Edit Undo command.

Working with Documents

ACT! saves your contact database when you make a change. With word processing documents, however, you must save the document. When you create a document, the text is stored only temporarily in the computer's memory. If something happens to the computer—if it is turned off accidentally or if you have a power outage—all information is lost unless you saved the document.

Saving a document writes the information from memory to disk. When you save the document the first time, you must assign a name. The next time(s) that you save, you don't need to enter the name.

You should save often—not just at the beginning of a document or at the end. If you save right after you start and don't save again for a long time, the disk version reflects only the changes you made *before* you saved. All later changes are lost if something happens to the computer. If you save only at the end, you risk losing all the information. Therefore, save every 10 or 15 minutes.

After you save the document, it is stored as a file on disk. You then can open and reuse the document, if needed.

Saving a Document

To save a document, follow these steps:

1. Choose the File Save command.

TIP: *Press Ctrl+S to choose the File Save command.*

You see the Save dialog box (see fig. 8.5). Here you assign a name and a directory for the document.

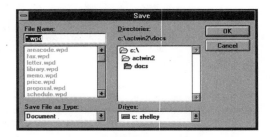

Figure 8.5. Saving a document.

2. In the File Name text box, type a file name.

    You can type up to eight characters. Don't assign an extension. ACT! assigns the extension WPD for all word processing documents.

    By default, ACT! stores all word processing documents in the directory C:\ACT2WIN\DOCS. To save the file in another drive or directory, follow step 3. Otherwise, skip to step 4.

3. To save the file to another directory, double-click on the directory name in the Directories list. To save the file to another drive, display the Drives drop-down list, and then click on the drive you want.

    If you want to take the file with you—perhaps to use on another computer—save the file to a floppy drive. If you use a different file organization, you may want to save the document to another directory. Chapter 12, "Customizing ACT!," explains the default file organization as well as how to change this organization.

4. Choose OK.

ACT! saves the document and displays the file name in the title bar of the document window.

The following checklist summarizes other save options:

✔ To save an existing document with a new name, choose the File Save As command. Type a new name and choose OK. Now, you have two versions of the file—the original file and the file saved with the new name.

✔ If you type the name of a file that already exists, you are asked whether you want to replace the existing file. Choose Yes to replace the disk file with the on-screen version. If you don't want to replace the file, choose No and type another file name.

✔ To save part of a document, select the text you want to save. Choose the File Save Selection As command. You see the Save As dialog box. Type a file name and choose OK. The selected text is saved in a file on disk.

✔ If you make changes in a document that you don't want to save, you can go back to the last saved version. Choose the File Revert command. When prompted whether you want to discard all changes, choose Yes. Keep in mind that *all* changes you made after the last save are lost.

Moving Among Documents

If you need to return to the contact screens—for example, to get information about a contact—open the Window menu. At the bottom, you should see the name of the contact database. Click on this name to return to the database. Open the Window menu and choose the document name to return to the document.

Closing a Document

When you finish working on a document, you can close it. First, save the document. If you try to close without saving, ACT! reminds you that you have not saved. Getting into the habit of saving before you close is a good idea.

To close a document, choose the File Close command or press Ctrl+W. ACT! closes the window and returns you to the contact database.

> **TIP:** *For information on deleting a document, see Chapter 13, "Maintaining the Database."*

Opening a Document

When you want to work on a document again—print it, make changes, add information, and so on—use the File Open command.

> **NOTE:** *If you are not in the word processing program and choose File Open, you see database files listed. To open another file type, display the List Files of Type drop-down list and select the kind of file that you want to open—for example, document. ACT! lists files of the type selected.*

Follow these steps:

1. Choose the File Open command.

   You see the Open File dialog box (see fig. 8.6).

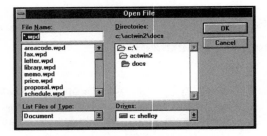

Figure 8.6. The Open File dialog box.

> **TIP:** *Press Ctrl+O to choose the File Open command.*

2. In the File Name list, click on the file you want to open.

   You can use the scroll arrows to scroll through the list.

3. Choose the OK button.

ACT! displays the document on-screen.

> **TIP:** *To combine two documents, open the first document. Place the insertion point at the spot you want to insert the second document. Then choose the File Insert command and choose the second document.*

Inserting Dates and Times

In letters, memos, and other documents, you may need to insert the current date. For time-sensitive projects, you also may want to include the time. ACT! provides a shortcut for entering both.

Inserting the Date

You can insert the date in one of two formats. You can insert the date as text—the date doesn't change—or you can insert a date that updates each time you open the document.

To insert the date, follow these steps:

1. Choose the Edit Insert Date command.

   You see the Insert Date dialog box (see fig. 8.7).

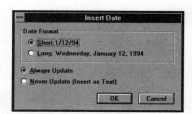

Figure 8.7. Inserting the date in a document.

2. Choose the date format you want: Short or Long.

   Short format lists the date in this format: 3/17/94. Long format uses this style: Thursday, March 17, 1994.

3. If you want the date to be updated each time you open the document, choose Always Update. Otherwise, choose Never Update.

   Always Update is useful when you are working on a document over·a period of time and want to include the current date. For instance, you may spend a week working on a proposal. When you insert the date and choose Always Update, ACT! updates the date each time you work on it. When you print the report, the date you printed is the date used in the report.

> **TIP:** *If you include the date in a template, use Always Update. Using this option ensures that the current date is inserted when you use the template. Chapter 9 discusses templates in more detail.*

Use Never Update to *freeze* the date. If you create a letter, for example, you want to have a record of when the letter was sent. Therefore, you do not want the date updated, so you choose Never Update.

4. Choose OK.

The date is inserted in the document. To delete the date, just select the inserted date and press Del.

Inserting the Time

If you need to time-stamp a document, use the Edit Insert Time command. You can choose to have the time updated or you can insert the time as regular text. Follow these steps:

1. Choose the Edit Insert Time command.

   You see the Insert Time dialog box (see fig. 8.8).

Figure 8.8. Inserting the time in a document.

2. If you want the time to update each time you open the document, choose Always Update. Otherwise, choose Never Update.

   Use Never Update to insert the current time; the time is not updated. Choose Always Update when you want the time to update each time you open the document.

> **NOTE:** *ACT! uses the date and time of your computer system's clock. If this clock is incorrect, you can update it using the Date/Time Control Panel in Windows. Open the Main program group; then double-click Control Panel. Double-click the Date/Time icon and then enter the correct date and time.*

3. Choose OK.

The Time is inserted in the document. To delete the Time, just select it and press Del.

Finding and Replacing Text

If you work in a long document and want to move quickly to a certain spot, you can spend a lot of time manually scanning for the spot for which you are looking. Instead, you can search for a word or phrase in the section you want, and then move to this spot quickly.

You also can search for and replace text in a document. Suppose that you use the term *spokesman* in your document and decide that *spokesperson* is a better word. Rather than finding each occurrence and changing it manually, you can have ACT! make the replacements.

Finding Text

When you want to move quickly to a section of a document, use the Find/Replace command. Follow these steps:

1. Choose the Edit Find/Replace command.

   You see the Find/Replace dialog box (see fig. 8.9).

2. In the Find What text box, type the text you want to find.

   You can type a phrase, a word, or part of a word.

> **TIP:** *Be as specific as possible when typing a search phrase. If you type a common word, you have to continue searching through all occurrences until you find the location you want. Pick a word or phrase unique in the section you want to find.*

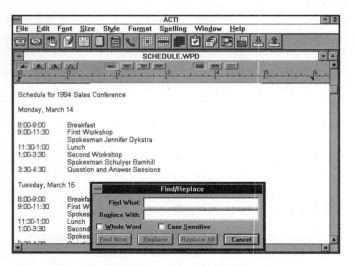

Figure 8.9. The Find/Replace dialog box.

3. If you want to find only whole words, check the Whole Word option.

    When this option is not selected, ACT! stops on the characters you enter, whether these characters are a word or part of a word. If you search for *arch*, for example, ACT! will stop on *arch*, *search*, *archway*, and so on. When Whole Word is checked, ACT! will stop only on *arch*.

4. If you want to match the case as you have typed it, check the Case Sensitive check box.

    By default, ACT! stops on each occurrence of the search string, regardless of case. For example, if you search for *Pam*, ACT! stops on *pam*, *PAM*, and *Pam*. If you want to stop only on *Pam*, type Pam and check the Case Sensitive check box.

5. Choose the Find Next button.

    ACT! moves to and selects the first occurrence of the text (see fig. 8.10). The dialog box remains open on-screen. To move to the next occurrence, choose the Find Next button again. To close the dialog box, choose the Cancel button.

If ACT! cannot find a match, you see an error message. Choose OK and check your spelling. If the spelling is correct, try searching for another word or phrase in the section you want to find.

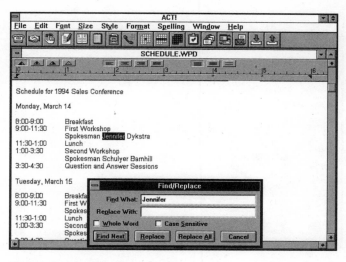

Figure 8.10. The found text.

Replacing Text

In addition to its other uses, the Find/Replace command can find a phrase or word and replace it with another. Follow these steps:

1. Choose the Edit Find/Replace command.

    You see the Find/Replace dialog box.

2. In the Find What text box, type the text you want to find.

    You can type a phrase, a word, or part of a word.

3. In the Replace With text box, type the text you want to use as the replacement.

    Again, you can type a phrase, a word, or part of the word. You can even leave the box blank to replace the text with nothing.

4. Check any of the following options:

    If you want to find only whole words, check the Whole Word option.

    If you want to match the case as you have typed it, check the Case Sensitive check box.

5. Choose the Find Next button.

    ACT! moves to and selects the first occurrence of the text (see fig. 8.11).

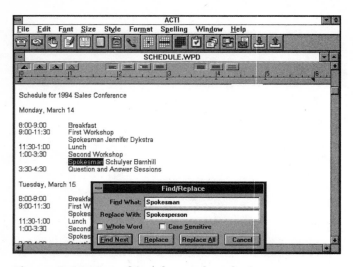

Figure 8.11. Searching for and replacing text.

You can choose to skip this instance, replace this instance, replace all instances, or cancel the operation.

6. Do one of the following:

   To skip this occurrence and move to the next one, choose the Find Next button.

   To make this replacement, choose the Replace button. Then choose the Find Next button to move to the next one.

   To replace all occurrences, choose the Replace All button.

   To cancel the operation, choose the Cancel button.

7. Continue confirming or canceling all replacements until you reach the end of the document. Choose Cancel to close the dialog box.

Checking Your Spelling

No matter how well-written or organized it is, your document will look unprofessional if a typo or misspelled word slips through. You can use ACT!s spell checker to check your spelling.

NOTE: *A spell check cannot take the place of a careful proofread. The spell checker doesn't know whether you mean to, two, or too; it just knows that*

> *all three are spelled correctly. Read all documents carefully before you send them out.*

Choosing Dictionaries

A spelling program works by comparing the words in your document to words in the program's dictionary. Before you can spell check a document, you need to select the main and user dictionary. ACT! uses the words in these documents to do the comparison. The main dictionary provided with ACT! is ENGLISH.DCT. You also can use the default user dictionary DEFAULT.USR. See the section "Working with User Dictionaries" for more information.

Choosing the Main Dictionary

The main dictionary is a dictionary provided with ACT! that contains a list of common words. You must choose a main dictionary. To choose the main dictionary, follow these steps:

1. Choose the Spelling Choose Main Dictionary command.

   You see the Choose Main Dictionary dialog box (see fig. 8.12). Here you select the dictionary you want to use. The dictionary provided with ACT! is named ENGLISH.DCT and is kept in the C:\ACTWIN2\SPELL directory.

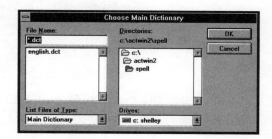

Figure 8.12. Choosing the main dictionary.

2. Click on the dictionary name and choose OK. You are returned to the document.

Choosing a User Dictionary

A user dictionary contains words that you add—for instance, proper names, terms, and other words that you want the spell checker to recognize. To choose a user dictionary, follow these steps:

1. Choose the Spelling Choose User Dictionary command.

    You see the Choose User Dictionary dialog box, which is similar to the dialog box shown in figure 8.12.

2. Click on the dictionary you want to use and choose OK.

You can double-click on the name to select the dictionary and close the dialog box. If you want to use the default dictionary, choose the DEFAULT.USR dictionary.

Checking Spelling

After you select the dictionaries, you can check your spelling. Follow these steps:

1. Choose the Spelling Check Document command.

    ACT! compares the words in your document to the words in the dictionaries and stops on any words it cannot find. You see the Spell Check dialog box (see fig. 8.13).

Figure 8.13. The Spell Check dialog box.

TIP: *To check just part of your document, select the part you want to check. Then choose the Spelling Check Selection command.*

---

2. Do one of the following for each of the words flagged:

    If the word is spelled correctly, choose the Skip button to skip this word and move to the next word.

If the word is spelled correctly and you want to add the word to your user dictionary, choose the Add button.

If the word is misspelled and the correct spelling is listed in the Suggestions list, click on the correct spelling. Then choose the Replace button.

If the word is misspelled, but the correct spelling is not listed, type the correct spelling in the Replace With text box. Then choose the Replace button.

After all words are checked, you see a dialog box showing the number of words checked and the number of misspelled words found.

3. Choose OK.

You are returned to the document.

Using a User Dictionary

When ACT! stops on a word that is misspelled, you can add the word to the dictionary. When you do so, ACT! doesn't flag the word as misspelled. You can gradually create a user dictionary by adding words as they come up. You may want to add names, terms, and abbreviations common to your business to the dictionary so that these words are not flagged.

If you add an incorrectly spelled word to the dictionary or if you want to manually add words, you can do so by editing the user dictionary. First, make sure that you selected the dictionary. See the section "Choosing Dictionaries." Then follow these steps:

1. Choose the Spelling Edit User Dictionary command.

    You see the User Dictionary dialog box (see fig. 8.14).

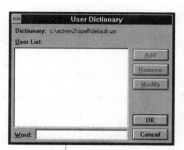

Figure 8.14. Editing the user dictionary.

2. Do any of the following:

   ✔ To delete a word from the dictionary, click on the word. Then choose the Remove button.

   ✔ To add a word, choose the Add button. Type the word you want to add and choose OK.

   ✔ To modify a word, click on the word in the list. Then choose the Modify button. Retype the word and choose OK.

3. When you are finished editing the dictionary, choose OK.

Q&A

I get an error message when I try to search for text in my document. What am I doing wrong?

If you get an error message, choose OK and try the following:

✔ Check your spelling. If you made a mistake when typing, retype the search phrase and try the search again.

✔ Be sure that you do not limit the search by choosing the Case Sensitive or Whole Word options. For example, if you search for Civil War, type **civil war**, and check the Case Sensitive check box. ACT! cannot find the occurrence, even though it is in the document.

I use certain technical terms that ACT! thinks are misspelled. Is there any way to stop ACT! from flagging these words?

✔ You can add words to your user dictionary so that ACT! does not flag them as misspelled. Choose the Add button when ACT! flags the word during a spell check. You also can manually add the words. See the section "Using a User Dictionary."

I deleted something by accident. Can I get the text back?

✔ If you realize you deleted text by accident, you can choose Edit Undo to undo the deletion. You must do this immediately after the deletion—before you perform any other task.

I inserted the date in a document, but the date keeps changing. How can I fix this?

✔ You can choose to insert a date that is updated automatically or one that is regular text. When you want the date to remain unchanged, be sure to choose the Never Update option.

Formatting Documents

Changing the look of a document is known as *formatting*. You have great control over the appearance of your documents—both letters and reports. You can change the font, add headers and footers, and more. This chapter covers the following formatting features:

- Changing the font
- Setting paragraph formats
- Setting tabs
- Setting page formats
- Adding headers and footers
- Creating templates
- Printing

Time-Management Tip

If you have trouble getting your day started, plan and complete an easy task first. That item doesn't need to be the most important item of the day. Completing an easy item will build your confidence and help you gain momentum for other tasks.

Changing the Font, Style, and Size

Words aren't the only way to convey meaning in a document. You can also use subtle formatting to affect the meaning. For instance, you can use bold type for information you want to stand out. You can use a large type size for the document heading.

What is a Font?

A font is a set of characters and numbers in a certain style. Times New Roman is one font. Courier is another font. Fonts have different characteristics. Here are some key concepts:

- ✔ *In a serif font, the characters have serifs, small bars or curls at the end of the character strokes.*

- ✔ *In a sans serif font, the characters don't have serifs. They consist of simple lines.*

- ✔ *Some fonts, such as Symbol and WingDings, contain different symbols such as ™ and ©.*

- ✔ *You can change the style of a font; for instance, make it bold or italic.*

- ✔ *Fonts are measured in points. There are 72 points in an inch. You can change the font size by selecting a different point size.*

- ✔ *Your printer has a number of built-in fonts. In the list of fonts, fonts with a little printer symbol next to them are printer fonts. With some printers, you can add more fonts, usually by inserting a font cartridge. Windows provides a new font technology, called TrueType. You can use any TrueType font installed through Windows. (Use the Control Panel to copy the font files to your disk.) TrueType fonts are indicated with TT in the Font list. Some programs come with a set of fonts. These fonts, also stored in files, are available as well.*

Here are some examples of common fonts:

Times New Roman

Palatino

Courier

Bookman

ZapfChancery

Shelley

Changing the Font Style

If you want the information in your document to stand out, consider applying a font style. You can make text bold, italic, and underlined. You can also change the color.

Follow these steps to change the font style:

1. Highlight the text you want to change.

   Remember to highlight or select text you drag across it with the mouse. You can also press and hold down the Shift key and use the cursor movement keys to highlight the text.

2. Open the Style menu.

   You see a list of Style options (see fig. 9.1).

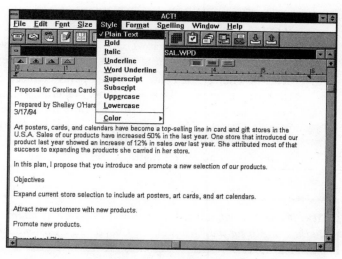

Figure 9.1. The Style menu choices.

3. Click on the style you want:

Option	Description
Plain Text	The default. Select when you have applied other styles and want to get rid of them—that is, return to plain text.
Bold	The most common formatting option. Useful for making document headings stand out. Keep in mind that too much bold can distract the reader.
Italic	Another way to make text stand out. Italic is often used for foreign phrases or for introducing new terms. Keep in mind that reading large blocks of italicized type can be difficult on the eyes.
Underline	Often used for book and other titles.
Word Underline	If you want to underline just the words—not the spaces between the words—choose this option.
Superscript	Often used in mathematical formulas and footnotes.
Subscript	Often used in mathematical equations.
Uppercase	Select to convert text to uppercase.
Lowercase	Select to convert text to lowercase. This option is useful if you accidentally type a lot of text with the Caps Lock key on.
Color	Select to change the color of the text, and then select a color from the submenu: Black, Red, Blue, Magenta, Yellow, White, Green, or Cyan. Text prints in color only if you have a color printer. Colored text is useful for documents that you send electronically and that will be read on-screen—for example, a memo you send over e-mail.

> **TIP:** *If you use bold, italic, or underline often, consider adding custom icons to the icon bar for these features. See Chapter 12, "Customizing ACT!".*

Figure 9.2 shows different type styles.

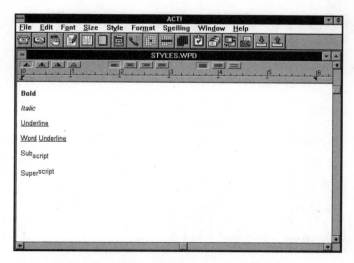

Figure 9.2. Examples of different type styles.

Changing the Font Size

The default font size is 10-point type, which may be too small and too hard to read. You can select a different font size. Making text larger—for example, making the document headings larger—helps give importance to the heading.

To change the font size, follow these steps:

1. Highlight the text you want to change.

2. Open the Size menu.

    You see a list of type sizes.

3. Choose the size you want.

To use a size not listed, choose Other and then type the size you want and choose OK. Figure 9.3 shows examples of different type sizes.

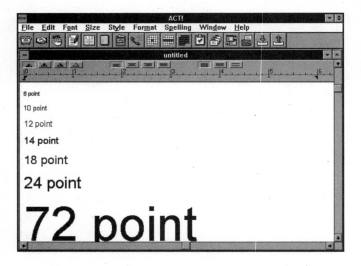

Figure 9.3. Different type sizes.

Changing the Font

Changing the style and size of the font is easiest using the Style and Size menus. When you want to change the font used or when you want to make several changes at once—for example, change the style, size, and font—use the Font dialog box.

To change the font, font size, and font style, follow these steps:

1. Choose the Font Choose command.

    You see the Font dialog box (see fig. 9.4).

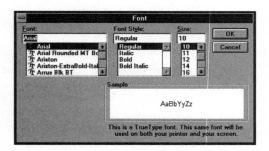

Figure 9.4. The Font dialog box.

2. In the Font list, click on the font you want to use.

   The fonts listed will depend on the printer you have and which fonts you have installed. You can click on the scroll arrows to scroll through the list. Notice that ACT! displays a sample of the selected font in the lower right corner.

3. In the Style list, click on the style you want.

   Depending on which font you have selected, the styles listed vary. The styles also are different from the styles listed on the Style menu.

4. In the Size list, click on the size you want.

   You can click on the scroll arrows to display additional sizes.

5. When you are finished making selections, choose OK.

ACT! formats the selected text with your new font, style, and size selections. Figure 9.5 shows a document that uses 12-point Times New Roman font.

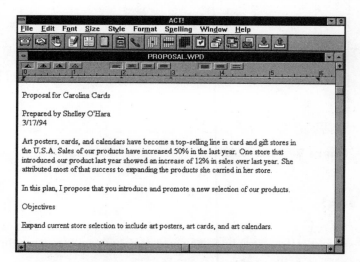

Figure 9.5. A document in 12-point Times New Roman font.

TIP: *To return the font to the default printer font, select the text. Then choose the Font Printer Default command.*

Setting Paragraph Formats

Paragraph formats include indenting, spacing, and alignment. You may want to indent the first line of your paragraphs, or you may want to switch from single to double-spacing. For document headings, you may want to center text. For return addresses, you may want to right-align the text. You can make all of these changes by using the Paragraph dialog box or the Ruler. Figure 9.6 identifies the Ruler icons and markers.

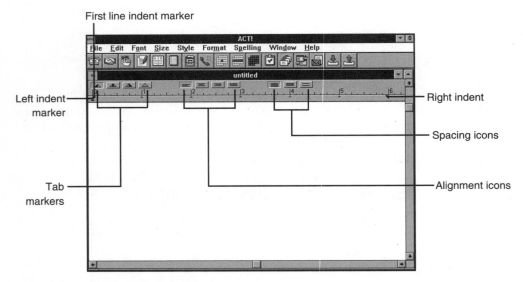

Figure 9.6. The Ruler.

Indenting Text

You can indent text from the left or right or both. You also can choose to indent just the first line of a paragraph. You can use either the Ruler or the Paragraph dialog box.

To indent a paragraph with the Ruler, drag the desired marker to the spot you want. You can drag the left indent marker (the first line indent marker moves with it), the right indent marker, or the first-line indent marker.

To indent text using the dialog box, follow these steps:

1. Highlight the text you want to indent.

   You can indent one paragraph or several. If you are indenting only one paragraph, you can just place the insertion point within the paragraph.

2. Choose the Format Paragraph command.

   You see the Paragraph dialog box (see fig. 9.7).

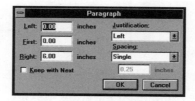

Figure 9.7. The Paragraph dialog box.

3. Do one of the following:

   To indent all lines from the left, enter a value in the Left and First text boxes. For example, to indent the lines by 1/4 inch, type *.25*.

   To indent only the first line, enter a value in the First text box.

   To create a hanging indent, enter a value in the Left text box.

   To indent from the right, enter a value in the Right text box.

4. Choose OK.

The paragraph is indented. Figure 9.8 shows examples of different indents.

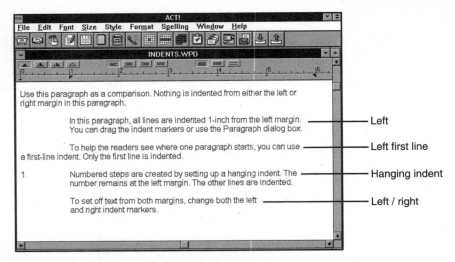

Figure 9.8. Examples of different indents.

Aligning Text

Besides indents, you can change the text alignment. Centered text often is used for headings or titles. Right-aligned text is useful for return addresses. You also can justify the text so that the left and right margins are even. You can use the ruler or the Paragraph dialog box to make the change.

To change the alignment by using the ruler, follow these steps:

1. Highlight the text you want to align.

   If you want to change just one paragraph, you can just place the insertion point within the paragraph. To change several paragraphs, select the ones you want to change.

2. Click on the alignment icon in the Ruler.

To use the dialog box, follow these steps:

1. Highlight the text you want to align.

2. Choose the Format Paragraph command.

   You see the Paragraph dialog box.

3. Display the Justification drop-down list and select the alignment you want.

   The default is Left. You can choose Left, Center, Right, or Full.

4. Choose OK.

Figure 9.9 shows some examples of different alignments.

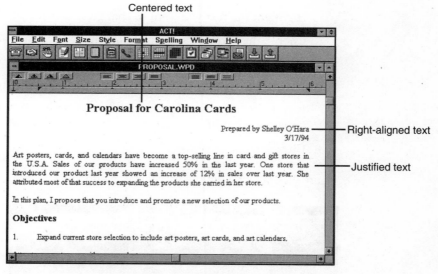

Figure 9.9. Examples of different alignments.

Changing Line Spacing

You can use the Ruler to change to double or 1 1/2 spacing. You can set the line spacing interval to any amount you want by using the dialog box.

To use the Ruler to change line spacing, follow these steps:

1. Highlight the text you want to change.

   To change just one paragraph, you can just place the insertion point within the paragraph. To change several paragraphs, select the ones you want to change.

2. Click on the spacing icon in the Ruler.

   Single

   1 1/2

   Double

To use the dialog box, follow these steps:

1. Highlight the text you want to change.

2. Choose the Format Paragraph command.

   You see the Paragraph dialog box.

3. Display the Spacing drop-down list and select a spacing interval.

   If you want to set an absolute amount, choose Absolute and then enter the amount you want in the text box below.

4. Choose OK.

Figure 9.10 shows a double-spaced paragraph.

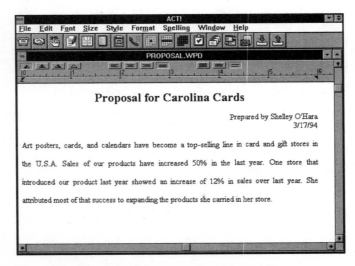

Figure 9.10. A double-spaced paragraph.

Setting Tabs

ACT! sets up tabs every inch. You can change the placement and the type of tabs, using the Ruler or the Tab dialog box. Using the Ruler, you see the changes immediately. The Tab dialog box is useful when you want to enter a precise measurement or when you want to use a fill character.

Setting Tabs with the Ruler

The following table shows the different tab types and their Ruler marker.

Tab Marker	Description
▲	Left-align tab
▲	Center-align tab
▲	Right-align tab
△	Decimal-align tab

To set a tab, drag the appropriate tab marker onto the Ruler. Then drag the marker to the position you want. To remove a tab, drag it off the Ruler.

Using the Tab Dialog Box

The Tab dialog box enables you to specify a *fill character*, a character that is repeated in between tabs. Fill characters are useful for creating dotted lines, as in a table of contents or in creating blank lines as in a form.

To set tabs with the Tab dialog box, follow these steps:

1. Highlight the paragraphs that you want to change.

   Each paragraph can have its own tab settings. If you want to apply the tab settings to the entire document, open the Edit menu and choose the Select All command.

2. Open the Format menu and choose the Tabs command.

   You see the Tabs dialog box (see fig. 9.11).

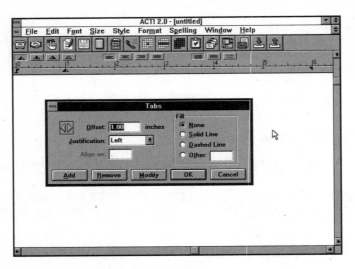

Figure 9.11. The Tabs dialog box.

3. Type the location for the first tab in the Offset text box. Type this location in inches.

4. Display the Justification drop-down list and select a tab type.

   You can choose Left, Right, Center, or Align. If you choose Align, enter the align character in the Align on text box.

5. If you want a fill character, select it in the Fill area.

   Fills are useful for creating forms (use the solid line), coupons (use the dashed line), or price lists (use a period). To use a different character, select Other and type the character in the text box.

6. Choose the Add button to add the tab.

   You can continue adding tabs or close the dialog box.

7. Choose OK to close the dialog box.

Figure 9.12 shows examples of different tab types.

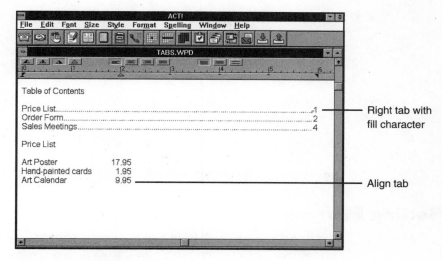

Figure 9.12. Tab types.

You also can use the Tabs dialog box to remove or modify tabs. In the Offset text box, type the tab marker you want to delete or change. To remove the tab, choose the Remove button. To modify the tab, make changes to the offset, alignment, or leader, and then choose the Modify button.

Copying Paragraph Formatting

The alignment, spacing, and tab settings are applied only to the selected paragraphs—not the entire document. If you've made changes to one paragraph and want to use the same settings in another paragraph, you can copy the formatting. The following paragraph formats are copied:

- ✔ Indents
- ✔ Alignment
- ✔ Line spacing
- ✔ Tabs

To copy paragraph formatting, follow these steps:

1. Put the insertion point in the paragraph that is formatted as you want.

   This paragraph contains the paragraph formats that you will copy.

2. Choose the Format Copy Ruler command.

   Nothing changes on-screen.

3. Click in the paragraph that you want to format with the copied settings.

   If you want to copy the formatting to several paragraphs, you can select them for this step.

4. Choose the Format Apply Ruler command.

The paragraph is formatted with the settings of the original paragraph.

Setting Margins

ACT! uses a 1-inch top and bottom margin and a 1.25 left and right margin. For most documents, these settings will work fine. If needed, you can change the settings. If you prefer more white space, you can increase the margins. If you are trying to fit a lot on a page, you can decrease the margins.

Follow these steps to change the margins:

1. Choose the Format Pages command.

   You see the Page Margins dialog box (see fig. 9.13).

Figure 9.13. The Page Margins dialog box.

2. Enter new values in the Top, Bottom, Left, or Right text boxes.

   Type the values in inches.

3. Choose OK.

The document is formatted with the new margins.

> **NOTE:** *You may get confused when you look at the Ruler and think that 0 is the edge of the page. 0 is the start of the text area. The negative values on the margin indicate the margin area.*

Adding Headers and Footers

For long documents, especially reports, you may want to include some kind of identification on all pages. For example, you may want to include the report name or the page number. Information that you want repeated at the top of all pages is called a *header*. Information repeated at the bottom of all pages is called a *footer*. You can create and use both headers and footers in your document.

To create a header or footer, follow these steps:

1. Choose the Format Insert Header command to create a header; choose the Format Insert Footer command to create a footer.

   ACT! moves you to the top of the document for headers or to the bottom for footers.

2. Type the information you want to include.

You can use any editing and formatting features in the header or footer text. To return to the document area, click within that area. Figure 9.14 shows a header with the proposal name and page number.

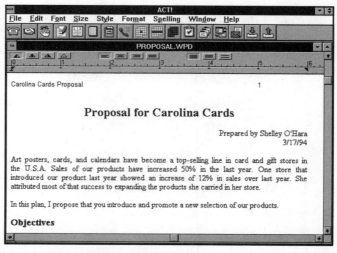

Figure 9.14. A sample header.

> **TIP:** *If you want to number pages, create a header or footer and insert the page number. To insert the page number, choose the Edit Insert Page Number command.*

The menus change when you are within a header or footer. Here are some other changes you can make to headers and footers:

✔ To remove a header or footer, click within the header or footer area. Then choose the Format Remove Header command or Format Remove Footer command.

✔ To change the amount of space between the header and the document text or the footer and the document area, click within the header or footer area. Then choose the Format Header Height or the Format Footer Height command. You see the Set Height dialog box. Type the amount of space you want to reserve for the header or footer. Then choose OK.

Printing

After you add the finishing touches to your document or report, you can print it. Information on setting up the printer is included in Appendix A.

Printing a Document

Follow these steps to print a document:

1. Choose the File Print command.

    You see the Print dialog box (see fig. 9.15).

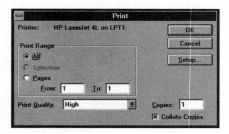

Figure 9.15. The Print dialog box.

> **TIP:** *Press Shift+F11 to choose the File Print command.*

2. Do any of the following:

   If you want to print more than one copy, enter the number of copies in the Copies text box.

   To print a range of pages, choose the Pages option and enter the page range you want to print.

   To change the print quality, display the Print Quality drop-down list and select a print quality.

3. Choose OK.

ACT! prints the document.

Deferring a Print Job

If you want to print a document or report at a later date or time, you can defer the print job. Follow these steps:

1. Choose the File Deferred Print command.

   You see the Deferred Print dialog box (see fig. 9.16).

Figure 9.16. Deferring a print job.

2. Enter a description of the print job and choose OK.

   You can set up several deferred print jobs. Use this description to remind yourself which print job is which.

The next time you start ACT! you will see a message reminding you that you have pending print jobs. Choose Yes to display the Deferred Print dialog box (see fig. 9.17).

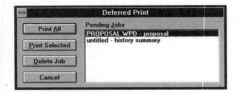

Figure 9.17. This dialog box lists the print jobs you have waiting.

You can do any of the following:

✔ To print all jobs, choose the Print All button.

✔ To print a job, click on the job in the list. Then choose the Print Selected button.

✔ To delete a job, click on the job in the list. Then choose the Delete Job button.

Q&A

How do I undo formatting changes?

✔ If you make a change and don't like it, choose Edit Undo immediately. Remember, though, that Undo can undo only the last command. If you made changes to the font style, you can choose Style Plain Text to return to regular text. If you made any other formatting changes and Undo isn't available, follow the same steps you made when you made the change, but this time select the original settings and choose OK.

How come I have different fonts than shown in the dialog box in this book?

✔ Each computer can have different fonts. The fonts depend on what type of printer you have and what fonts you have installed through Windows. You can purchase many different kinds of additional fonts.

How do I print a deferred print job?

✔ The only opportunity you have to print deferred jobs is when you start ACT! Each time you start the program, you will be reminded of any pending print jobs. Exit and restart ACT! when you want to print the deferred jobs.

Creating Letters, Memos, and Faxes

The word processor is a great tool for creating proposals and reports, but ACT! has done more than provide these features. ACT! includes some predefined document formats that you can use to create a letter, memo, and fax quickly. ACT! automatically fills in key information—for example, the contact name and address—and formats the letter in a professional style.

This chapter covers the following topics:

• Creating a letter

• Creating a memo

• Creating a fax cover sheet

> **NOTE:** *For complete information on all editing and formatting features, see Chapters 8 and 9.*

Creating a Letter

Letters are useful for following up a call and confirming in writing any agreements or scheduled meetings. You also may want to send letters to clients, thanking them for an order. ACT! makes creating and printing a letter easy.

To create a letter, follow these steps:

1. Display the contact to whom you want to send the letter.

    ACT! pulls key information from the contact screen—the contact name, company name, address, and salutation (the *Dear* field). This is the reason you first display the contact to whom you are sending the letter.

2. Choose the Write Letter command.

   ACT! inserts the date, contact name and address, salutation, and closing (see fig. 10.1).

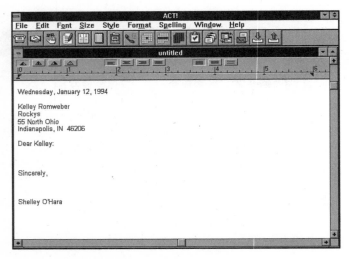

Figure 10.1. Creating a letter.

3. Click in the empty space below the salutation and type the text of the letter.

   You can use any of the formatting and editing techniques described in Chapters 8 and 9. For instance, you may want to use a different font or italicize a key date.

4. After you finish creating the letter, choose the File Save command, type a file name, and choose OK.

   You don't have to save the file; you can just print it. But if something goes wrong during the print job and the document is lost, you need to recreate the letter, which is why saving the letter before you print is usually a good idea.

5. Choose the File Print command.

You see the Print dialog box (see fig. 10.2).

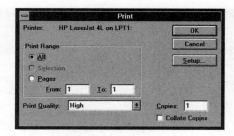

Figure 10.2. The Print dialog box.

6. Choose OK.

   ACT! prints the letter and displays a dialog box asking whether this is a letter that you want to send.

7. Choose Yes if this is a finished letter; No if it is a rough draft.

   If you choose Yes, ACT! updates the Letter Date and Letter Name fields on the contact database screen. If you choose No, a draft is printed, but the fields are not updated.

   You are asked whether you want to print an envelope.

8. Choose Yes to print an envelope. When you see the Print dialog box, choose OK to print the envelope. Otherwise, choose No.

If you request it, ACT! prints the envelope and updates the Letter Date and Letter Name fields, if necessary (see fig. 10.3). Figure 10.4 shows a printed letter.

Creating a Memo

Memos are just as easy to create. ACT! will enter a memo heading, the date, the contact name, and your name. Follow these steps:

1. Display the contact to which you want to send the memo.

   ACT! pulls the contact name from the record.

2. Choose the Write Memorandum command.

   ACT! inserts the date, contact name, and your name (see fig. 10.5).

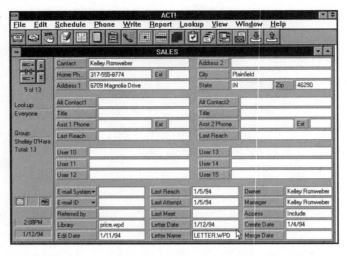

Figure 10.3. The letter fields are updated when you send a letter.

Wednesday, January 12, 1994

Kelley Romweber
Rockys
55 North Ohio
Indianapolis, IN 46206

Dear Kelley:

Thanks for your recent order. The shipment should be arriving in the next 7 to 10 business days.
If you have any problems with the order, please give me a call at (317) 555-9001.

I look forward to seeing you on March 17 for our sales meeting.

Sincerely,

Shelley O'Hara

Figure 10.4. A printed letter.

3. Type the subject, press Enter, and type the text for the memo.

   You can use any formatting and editing technique described in
   Chapters 8 and 9. For example, you may want to use a different font
   or italicize a key date.

4. After you finish creating the memo, choose the File Save command,
   type a file name, and choose OK.

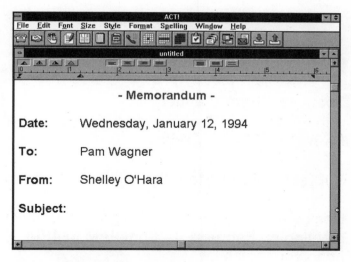

Figure 10.5. Creating a memo.

You don't have to save the file; you can just print it. But if something goes wrong during the print job and the document is lost, you'll have to recreate the memo again—possibly from scratch, which is why saving and then printing the memo is usually a good idea. If you save the memo, you also can refer to the file later, if needed, to discuss any key points with the contact.

5. Choose the File Print command.

   You see the Print dialog box.

6. Choose OK.

   ACT! prints the memo and displays a dialog box asking whether this is a finished document that will be sent out.

7. Choose Yes if you plan to send the memo, No if the memo is only a draft.

If you choose Yes, ACT! updates the Letter Date and Letter Name fields on the contact database screen. If you choose No, a draft is printed, but the fields are not updated. Figure 10.6 shows a printed memo.

- Memorandum -

Date: Wednesday, January 12, 1994

To: Pam Wagner

From: Shelley O'Hara

Subject: Sales Meeting

Don't forget that we are holding our monthly sales meeting on February 14 from 9AM to 4PM. Please bring your sales kit.

The meeting will be held at the Atlas Conference Center. A map is attached.

See you on the 14th.

Figure 10.6. A printed memo.

Creating and Sending a Fax

Creating a fax cover sheet is simple when you use ACT!. If you have a fax/modem, you can fax right from your computer. To create and send a fax, follow these steps:

1. Display the contact to whom you want to send the fax.

   ACT! pulls the contact name and fax number from the record.

2. Choose the Write Fax Cover command.

   ACT! inserts the date, contact name, fax number, and your name (see fig. 10.7).

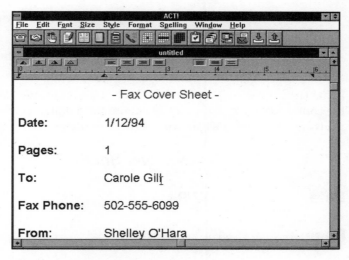

Figure 10.7. Creating a fax.

3. Type the subject of the fax, press Enter, and type any text you want to include on the cover sheet.

   You can use any formatting and editing technique described in Chapters 8 and 9. For instance, you can change the font, margins, or other formatting of the document.

4. Choose the File Save command, type a file name, and choose OK.

   If you don't want to save the file, you can skip this step.

5. Take one of the following actions:

   If you want to print a hard copy, choose the File Print command and choose OK.

   To fax the document, first choose the File Printer Setup command and then select the fax driver. Appendix A discusses how to set up a printer. Choose OK and then choose the File Print command. Follow the instructions for your particular fax program to complete the fax transmission.

NOTE: *If you want to fax from your computer, you need a fax/modem. When you install the fax/modem and communication software, the program creates the necessary printer driver.*

ACT! prints the fax and displays a dialog box, asking whether this is a finished document.

7. If you plan to send the fax, choose Yes; choose No if the fax is just a draft.

If you choose Yes, ACT! updates the Letter Date and Letter Name fields on the contact database screen. If you choose No, a draft is printed, but the fields are not updated. Figure 10.8 shows a printed memo.

- Fax Cover Sheet -

Date: 1/12/94

Pages: 1

To: Carole Gill

Fax Phone: 502-555-6099

From: Shelley O'Hara

Subject: Quote

The sales quote we discussed is attached for your review.

Figure 10.8. A printed fax cover sheet.

Q&A

When I send a fax, it prints on my printer. How do I fax it?

✔ To send a fax, you select the fax driver. A fax driver is similar to a printer driver; it tells the program key information about the hardware. See Appendix A for information about setting up a printer.

Can I change the letter or memo format so that I can use the same format again?

✔ If you don't like the template used for the letter, memo, or fax cover sheet, you can change the template. You also can create your own templates, as described in Chapter 10.

Creating Form Letters and Templates

If you need to send the same letter to several contacts, dont waste time creating individual letters. Instead, create a form letter. A form letter enables you to create one letter and then merge the letter with the contacts you want to create personalized letters for. Technically, a form letter is a template. This chapter covers form letters first and then discusses other template subjects.

The following topics are covered:

• Creating form letters

• Creating mailing labels

• Using ACT!'s templates

• Adding a template to the menu

Creating Form Letters

To create a form letter, you first set up a template. The template includes the text you want to include in the letter—the date, the letter contents, closing, and your name. You type this text just as you do in a normal document.

A template also includes field codes. These codes tell ACT! to pull information from the contact database. For example, you would include fields for the contact and company name, address, salutation, and so on.

After you create the template, you group the records you want to use. For example, to send the letter only to certain contacts, first create a group for those contacts. Then you merge and print the letters. This section describes all the steps needed to create a form letter.

Creating a Template

To begin, you create a letter template that includes the letter text and fields that indicate which information you want pulled from the contact database.

TIP: *It may be a good idea to sketch out your letter on paper or, using the word processor, do a rough draft. You then will know which fields you need to include and what you want to say.*

NOTE: *Follow these same steps to create any letter format. The example used here is for a form letter, but you can create an order form or any other letter template.*

To create a form letter, follow these steps:

1. Choose the File New command.

   You see the New File dialog box (see fig. 11.1).

Figure 11.1. The New File dialog box.

2. Choose Letter Template.

   You see a blank word processing document with the Field Names dialog box open at the bottom of the screen (see fig. 11.2).

3. Type the text of the letter.

   Type only the text that you want to appear in each letter—for instance, the date. Don't type information that you want to use from the contact database. Instead, insert a field code, as described in the next step.

4. When you want to insert a field, choose Contact Field in the Type area and then choose the field you want to insert from the Field list.

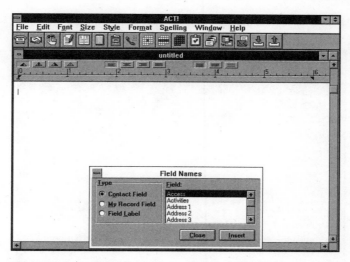

Figure 11.2. Creating a new letter template.

In reports, you often include the field label, but you usually don't include the labels in the letter. You can include information from your record by choosing the My Record option in the Type area and choosing the field you want from the Field list. For instance, you may want to insert your name and company name using the My Record fields.

> **NOTE:** *If you close the Field Names dialog box and need to reopen it, choose the Format Show Field Names command.*

You also can use any of the editing and formatting features of the word processing program. See Chapters 8 and 9 for more information on these features.

Saving the Template

When you have finished creating the letter template, you need to save it to disk. Follow these steps:

1. Choose the File Save command.

   You see the Save dialog box (see fig. 11.4). Notice that ACT! uses the extension TPL for templates and stores the templates in the C:\ACTWIN2\TEMPLATE directory.

Figure 11.3 shows a completed form letter.

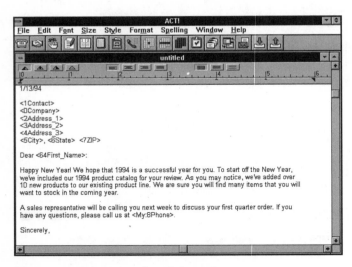

Figure 11.3. A completed form letter.

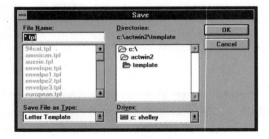

Figure 11.4. Saving the letter template.

2. Type a file name and choose OK.

    You can type up to eight characters for the file name. Use a name that reminds you of the purpose of the template. For example, if the form letter was to introduce your 1994 catalog, you might name the template 94CAT. ACT! saves the template and displays the file name in the title bar. You can close the file (choose File Close) to return to the contact database.

> **TIP:** *To test the merge, choose the Format Merge Template command. Then choose OK. Make sure that you inserted all the fields and that you inserted all necessary spaces and returns. For example, you need to type a comma between city and state and include two spaces after state. If necessary, make any corrections, and then close the file.*

Printing the Form Letters

If you want to send the form letter to all contacts, look up everyone. In some cases, you may want to send the letter to just a group of contacts. In this case, create a lookup group with the contacts you want. Chapter 3, "Managing Contacts," covers lookup groups in more detail.

When you are ready to create and print the form letters, follow these steps:

1. Choose the Write Form Letter command.

   You see the Select Form Letter command (see fig. 11.5). ACT! lists all the letter templates on the drive. Notice that ACT! provides some templates that you can use. See the section "Using and Creating Templates" for information about other templates.

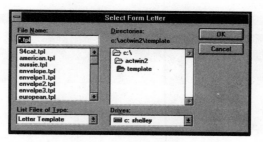

Figure 11.5. Selecting the form letter file.

2. Click on the form letter file and choose OK.

   ACT! displays the Prepare Form Letter dialog box (see fig. 11.6).

Figure 11.6. The Prepare Form Letter dialog box.

3. If you want to change which contacts are included, select another option in the Use area: Active Contact, Active Lookup, or All Contacts.

   The Use default is Active Lookup. The default for output is Document—that is, the form letters will be displayed on-screen. Usually, viewing the letters first to make sure that they are correct is a good idea. You then can print from the resulting document. If you are positive the template is correct, choose Printer.

4. Choose OK.

ACT! creates a personalized letter for each contact (see fig. 11.7). If you need to keep a copy of the letters, save the document by using the File Save command. Then print the letters.

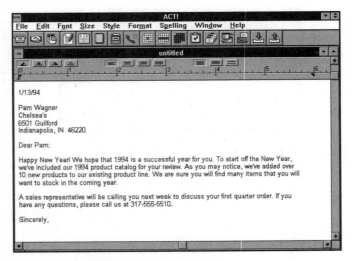

Figure 11.7. The final form letter.

If the letters are acceptable, print them, as described in the following steps.

5. Choose the File Print command.

    You see the Print dialog box (see fig. 11.8).

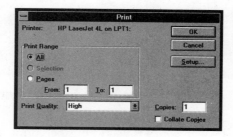

Figure 11.8. The Print dialog box.

6. Choose OK to print the documents.

    ACT! prints the letters and asks whether these are finished letters.

7. Choose Yes to update the Letter Date and Letter Name fields on the contact record. Otherwise, choose No.

You can then send out the personalized letters.

Creating Mailing Labels

Like form letters, mailing labels involve the use of a template. Labels use a report format. To create mailing labels, follow these steps:

1. Choose the Report Other command.

    You see the Select Report dialog box (see fig. 11.9). ACT! lists all the report templates (REP files). The AVRY files are label formats.

2. Choose the label format you want to use.

    If you purchase Avery labels, select the file name that matches the labels you purchased. The labels have a 4-digit product code. If you purchased another brand of label, look on the box. It probably states that the label is similar to an Avery style. If it doesn't, you have to experiment.

3. Choose OK.

    You see the Prepare Report dialog box.

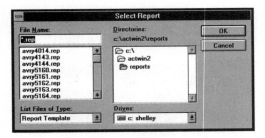

Figure 11.9. Selecting one of the label formats.

4. Select which contacts you want labels printed for: Active Contact, Active Lookup, All Contacts.

   The default is Active Lookup.

5. Choose OK.

ACT! displays the labels on-screen. If the labels look right, choose File Print, then choose OK to print the labels.

Using a Template

ACT! provides several templates that you can use to create form letters, order forms, and other document types. To use the template as the basis of a form letter, choose the Write Form Letter command. Then choose the template in the Select Form Letter dialog box. To use the template to create an individual letter, choose the Write Other command. In the Select Letter dialog box, select the template you want to use.

Table 11.1 lists the predefined letter templates.

Table 11.1. Letter Templates

File Name	Description
american.tpl	Business letter with day and date, contact name, address, salutation, and closing.
aussie.tpl	Business letter that conforms to Australian business standards.
envelope.tpl	Landscape business envelope.
envelope1.tpl	Portrait business envelope with a return address.
envelope2.tpl	Landscape business envelope with a return address.
envelope3.tpl	Portrait business envelope.
european.tpl	Memo with date, contact, title, address, and subject lines.

File Name	Description
fax.tpl	Fax cover sheet. This is the template that is used when you choose the Write Fax Cover command. See Chapter 10, "Creating Letters, Memos, and Faxes."
faxltr.tpl	Combination of fax.tpl and letter.tpl
letter.tpl	Business letter with day and date, contact name, address, salutation, and closing. This is the template that is used when you choose the Write Letter command. This feature is described in Chapter 10.
memo.tpl	Memo with title, date, contact name, your name, and subject line. This template is used when you choose Write Memo (see Chapter 10).
order.tpl	Creates an internal order form for sales personnel.
uk.tpl	Business letter that conforms to United Kingdom's business standards.

Figure 11.10 shows a document using faxltr.tpl, and figure 11.11 shows the order.tpl.

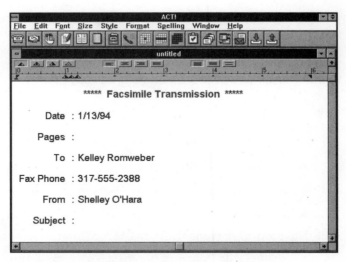

Figure 11.10. A different style fax sheet.

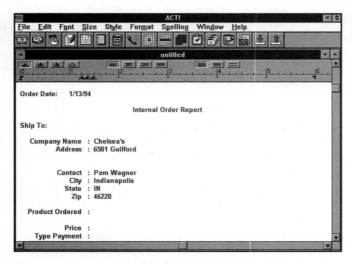

Figure 11.11. An order form.

Editing a Template

If you create a template and make a mistake or want to add text, you can edit the template. You also can edit the predefined templates, but if you do, use the File Save As command to save the template with a new name. Saving a template with a new name preserves the original template on disk so that you are sure to have an unmodified copy of it.

To edit a template, follow these steps:

1. Choose the Write Edit Template command.

   You see the Select Letter dialog box.

2. Click on the template you want to change and choose OK.

   ACT! displays the template on-screen.

3. Make any of the following changes:

   To add text, click where you want the new text and type.

   To format the template, select the text you want to change and then apply any of the font, style, or size features.

   To add a field, choose Contact Field in the Field Names dialog box. Then click on the field you want in the Field list.

For more information on editing and formatting features, see Chapters 8 and 9.

4. Choose the File Save command to save the template.

   The new template is saved to disk.

5. Choose the File Close command.

The template is closed. See the section "Using a Template" for information on how to use the modified template.

Adding a Template to the Menu

If you use a template often, you can add it to the Write menu.

To add a template to the Write menu, follow these steps:

1. Choose the Write Modify Menu command.

   You see the Custom Letter dialog box.

2. Choose the Add button.

   You see the Add Custom Menu Item dialog box (see fig. 11.12).

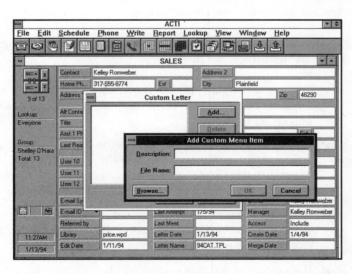

Figure 11.12. The Add Custom Menu Item dialog box.

3. Type the name you want to appear on the menu in the Description text box.

   For example, you might type Catalog for the Catalog letter.

4. In the File Name text box, type the name of the letter template.

   Type the same name you used when you saved the letter template. Be sure to type the extension, too.

TIP: *If you can't remember the name, click the Browse button. By default, ACT! stores all letter templates in the directory C:\ACTWIN2\TEMPLATES. You see the files in this directory. Double-click on the file name you want.*

---

5. Choose OK.

You are returned to the Custom Template dialog box. The new menu item is listed in the dialog box.

6. Choose OK.

You are returned to the contact screen.

The following checklist summarizes how to execute, rearrange, and delete a template from the Write menu:

✔ To use the template, choose the Write command. You should see the template name listed at the bottom of the menu. Click on it to select and create the letter.

✔ If you want to delete an item from the menu, choose the Write Modify Menu command. Click on the menu item you want to delete. Then click the Delete button. Keep in mind that this process deletes the menu item, but does not delete the template file stored on disk.

✔ If you have several menu items and want to rearrange them, choose the Write Modify Menu command. Click on the menu item you want to change. Then click Item Up or Item Down.

✔ If you want to separate queries by lines, choose the Write Modify Menu command. Click the Add Line button. A line is added above the current item. (You can adjust the placement of the line by clicking on it and clicking the Item Up or Item Down button.)

Q&A

Can I modify an existing template to create a new template?

✔ If you like one of the predefined templates provided with ACT!, you can start with that template and make changes to create a new template. For instance, you may want to start with the LETTER.TPL to create your form letter.

Be sure that you use the File Save As command to save the template with a new file name. Otherwise, you write over the original template on disk. You should keep the original files so that you have them if you need them.

Do all templates have to be form letters?

✔ No. The example of a form letter is used in this chapter to show you how to create a template. You follow the same steps to create any type of template.

You don't have to merge the template with other letters, either. To create a single letter based on the templates, display the contact you want and use the Write Other command instead of the Write Form Letters command.

PART

Customizing

Customizing ACT!

The programmers who created ACT! put some thought into how most people will use the program, and set default settings accordingly. For instance, ACT! sets up directories for each type of data file. Also, ACT! uses certain default settings for where the icon and status bar appear. If these settings don't match the way you prefer to work, you can change them.

Another way to customize ACT! is to create and use macros. You can create a macro to automate a task you do over and over. You can assign the macro to an icon, if you choose.

This chapter covers the following topics:

- Setting preferences
- Creating macros
- Using a description file

Setting Preferences

There are eleven categories of preferences, containing a range of default options. You can control options ranging from the default lead and duration time from a call to the default location for certain file types. This section covers most preference options. For information on Dialing Settings, see Appendix A. For information on custom icons, see the section on macros later in this chapter.

Generally, you make a change to the default settings by taking these steps:

1. Choose the Edit Preferences command.

    You see the Preferences dialog box.

2. In the Modify list, choose the setting you want to change.

   The options in the right side of the dialog box will vary depending on the selected option.

3. Make any changes and choose OK.

The dialog box is closed and the program updated to reflect your new selections. The following sections discuss the settings you can change in more detail.

Alarm Settings

Choose Alarm Settings to modify the default lead and duration time for calls, meetings, and to-do items. You also can use this option to control whether alarms are sounded and whether schedule conflicts are checked. Figure 12.1 shows the alarm settings you can change.

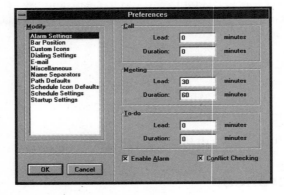

Figure 12.1. The Alarm Settings option.

You can change any of the following settings:

✔ To change the lead or duration time for calls, meetings, or to-dos, click in the appropriate text box and type a new value. The default for calls and to-dos is 0 for lead time and duration. The default for meetings is 30 (lead) and 60 (duration).

✔ You can control which activities have alarms by checking the Set Alarm check box when you schedule the activity. If you want to turn off all alarms, uncheck the Enable Alarm check box.

✔ If you schedule two activities at the same time, ACT! displays a conflict dialog box. If you don't want to be alerted when you have a schedule conflict, uncheck the Conflict Checking check box.

Bar Position

To control the placement of the icon and status bars, choose Bar Position. Figure 12.2 shows the Bar Position options.

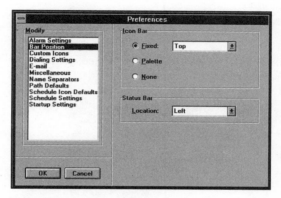

Figure 12.2. The Bar Position options.

To change the placement of the icon bar, take one of the following actions:

✔ Choose the Fixed option, display the drop-down list, and select a placement (Top, Bottom, Left, Right).

✔ Choose Palette. When you choose Palette, the icons are displayed in a palette on-screen. You can use the mouse to drag the palette wherever you want on-screen.

✔ To hide the icon bar, choose None.

To change the placement for the status bar, display the Location drop-down list and select a placement (Top, Bottom, Left, or Right).

Figure 12.3 shows the icon bar as a palette and the status bar at the right.

Figure 12.3. Changing the icon bar.

E-Mail

Choose E-mail to set e-mail options (see fig. 12.4). Then take any of the following actions:

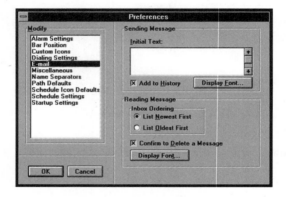

Figure 12.4. ACT!'s E-mail options.

✔ To enter an initial sending message, type it in the Initial Text box.

✔ If you want to add a record to the contact history for e-mail you send, check the Add to History check box.

✔ To change the order in which messages are displayed, select List Newest First or List Oldest First.

✔ To change the font for sending or receiving messages, click the Display Font button. Then choose a font, font size, and style you want.

✔ If you don't want ACT! to confirm each message deletion, uncheck the Confirm to Delete a Message check box.

Miscellaneous

To set miscellaneous options such as which key moves from field to field and whether the spell check suggests alternative spellings, choose Miscellaneous. Figure 12.5 shows the Miscellaneous options.

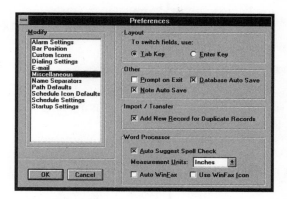

Figure 12.5. Miscellaneous options.

Make changes to any of the following options:

✔ If you prefer to press Enter to move from field to field, choose Enter key in the Layout area.

✔ By default, the database is saved after you make changes, and all notes are saved. To turn off these options, uncheck the Database Auto Save and/or Note Auto Save check boxes.

✔ If you want to display a prompt that says `Are you sure you want to exit` each time you choose the File Exit command, check the Prompt on Exit command.

✔ When you import new records to a database, ACT! creates a new record and keeps the original if it finds a duplicate record. Appendix B covers importing. If you want to overwrite duplicate records, uncheck the Add New Record for Duplicate Record check box.

✔ When you spell check a document, ACT! flags misspelled words and automatically suggests alternative spellings. Uncheck the Auto Suggest Spell Check check box if you don't want alternatives listed.

✔ The ACT! word processor uses inches as its default measurement. Display the Measurement drop-down list and choose another measurement, if you want.

✔ If you have WinFax 3.0 or above, check the Auto WinFax check box. If you do so, ACT! automatically supplies the contact name and fax number to word processing documents you want to fax. To include an icon for WinFax, check the Use WinFax Icon check box.

Name Separators

Name separators are used for two purposes. First, separators help ACT! separate a contact name into first and last names so that you can lookup on both. Second, they are used in word processing greeting lines ("Dear Mrs. Smith..."). You need to correctly identify any separators you want to use. ACT! sets up the most common first name (Miss, for example) and last name prefixes (Van Der) and last name suffixes (CPA, for example).

To review, add, or delete name separators, choose Name Separators. You see the Name Separators options (see fig. 12.6).

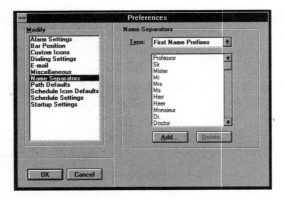

Figure 12.6. Name Separators options.

First, display the name separators you want to review or edit by displaying the drop-down list and selecting First Name Prefixes, Last Name Prefixes, or Last Name Suffixes.

To delete an item, click on the item in the list. Then choose the Delete button. To add an item, choose the Add button, type the separator, and choose OK.

Path Defaults

ACT! sets up *default directories* (places on your hard disk that hold categories of information) for the following file types: Database, Template, Docs, Reports, Macros, Queries, Layouts, Filters, Spell, ACT! Network, File Lock, Printout, Deferred, Mail, Outbox, and Bcase. To change the default directory, follow these steps:

1. In the Modify list, select Path Defaults.

   You see the Path Defaults options (see fig. 12.7).

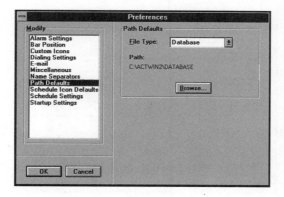

Figure 12.7. Path Defaults options.

2. Display the File Type drop-down list and select the type of file you want to change.

3. Choose the Browse button.

   You see the Choose Default Path dialog box.

4. Select the drive and directory you want to use for the new path.

5. Choose OK.

Schedule Icon Defaults

By default, the schedule icons schedule new calls, meetings, or to-dos. If you'd rather use these icons to modify calls, meetings, or to-dos, choose the Schedule Icon Defaults option. Then change the icons use for calls, meetings, and to-dos. Choose OK.

Schedule Settings

When you schedule an activity, certain options appear by default. For instance, an on-screen calendar pops up so that you can select the date. If you prefer to see another type of calendar or if you prefer not to display the popup, you can make a change.

Follow these steps to make a change:

1. Select Schedule Settings.

   You see the schedule options (see fig. 12.8).

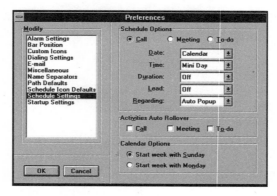

Figure 12.8. Schedule Settings.

2. Select the type of activity you want to change: Call, Meeting, or To-do.

   Click on the option button to make a selection. The same options are available for each.

3. Make any of the following option choices:

   To change how the Date will appear, display the Date drop-down list and choose an option (Calendar, Week View, Month View, Date/Time, or Off).

   To change how the time appears in the Time field, display the Time drop-down list and choose an option (Date/Time, Mini Day, Timeless, or Off).

   To change what appears for the Duration field, display the Duration drop-down list and choose Off or Date/Time.

To choose what appears for the Lead field, display the Lead drop-down list and choose Off or Date/Time.

To choose what appears for the Regarding field, display the drop-down list and choose Auto Popup or Off.

4. If you want ACT! to take any activities not completed and roll them over to the next day, check the activities you want rolled over (Calls, Meetings, or To-do).

You can check more than one option.

5. Check how you want your calendar to appear: Start week with Sunday or Start week with Monday.

6. Choose OK.

Startup Settings

If you want to run a macro, display a certain database file, or use a different library when you start ACT!, investigate the Startup Settings. Figure 12.9 shows the Startup Settings options.

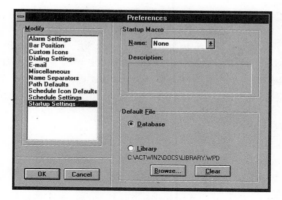

Figure 12.9. The Startup Settings options.

To change the Startup Settings options make any of the following choices:

✔ To have ACT! execute a macro on startup, enter the macro name in the Name box.

✔ To have ACT! display a database file, click the Database option button. Then choose the Browse button. Select the database you want opened each time you start ACT!

✔ To have ACT! use a different library file, click the Library option button. Then choose the Browse button. Select the WPD file you want to use. For more information on using libraries, see Chapter 2, "Setting up a Correct Database."

Creating Macros

Another way that you can customize ACT! is to create and use macros. Macros automate routine tasks—tasks that you perform over and over. For example, suppose that you often want to view your contact records sorted by last name. You can record a macro that sorts the records.

If you don't want to create macros, you may want to look into some of the macros provided with ACT! You can add these macros, or macros you create, to the icon bar.

Time-Management Tip

Learn to spot the time grabbers in your life. A time grabber could be a TV that is left on that lures you away from work, or a chatty co-worker. Make a plan for avoiding time grabbers. For instance, if you have a chatty co-worker, have a polite response ready for when that co-worker calls or stops by. You might say, for example, "I have to complete this project this morning, so I've got to get back to work."

Using ACT! Macros

ACT! provides several macros that you can use. The section on "Running Macros" covers how to run the macro. Table 12.1 lists the macros and their functions.

Table 12.1. ACT! Macros

Macro Name	Description
Bold	Apply bold
closedb	Close database
editlook	Edit current lookup
emailadr	Edit e-mail address
emailcr8	Create new e-mail
emaildis	Disconnect from e-mail
emailin	Open e-mail inbox
emailout	Open e-mail outbox
exit	Exit ACT! for Windows
fileopen	Open a database
Insert	Insert a new contact
Italic	Italic text
lookevry	Look up every contact
looklst	Look up on last name
lookmy	Look up my record
merge	Merge with another database
Normal	Normal type
Paste	Paste text
princal	Print calendar
prncont	Print contact report
prntaddr	Print address book
reflib	Display reference library
savecont	Save contact
savedoc	Save document
spellchk	Run spell check
timer	Start timer
undline	Underline text

Recording a Macro

To create a macro, turn on the recorder and perform the steps you want recorded. ACT! records these keystrokes, all mouse movements, or both. After you finish, you stop the recorder.

To record a macro, follow these steps:

1. Choose the Edit Macro command.

   You see a submenu of choices.

2. Choose the Record Macro command.

TIP: *You can press Alt+F5 to choose the Record Macro command.*

You see the Record Macro dialog box (see fig. 12.10).

Figure 12.10. The Record Macro dialog box.

Here you enter a name, a description, and tell ACT! what actions to record.

3. Type a name in the Name text box.

   The name can be up to eight characters long. Don't type an extension. ACT! assigns the extension MAC and stores the macro file in the C:\ACTWIN2\MACROS directory.

4. Type a description in the Description text box.

   By default, ACT! records only mouse actions, not keystrokes. If you want to change what is recorded, follow the next step. Otherwise, skip to step 6.

5. Display the Mouse drop-down list and select which options to record:

Option	Description
Record Clicks and Drags	Records only mouse actions
Record Everything	Records mouse and keyboard actions
Ignore Mouse	Records only keyboard actions

6. Choose the Record button.

   Nothing is displayed on-screen to remind you that you are recording a macro. Be careful! Everything you select, every command, mouse action, and key press is recorded until you stop the recorder.

7. Perform the actions you want to record.

   Go slow and be careful. You don't want to record the wrong actions in the macro. If you do, you'll have to start over.

8. When you are finished making selections, choose the Edit Macro Stop Recorder command.

The macro is recorded and ready for you to use again. The next section explains how to run a macro.

Running a Macro

When you want to perform the steps that you recorded in the macro, you simply play back the macro. First, make sure that the record or document you want to work with is displayed on-screen because ACT! will carry out the macro's commands on the current window. Then follow these steps:

1. Choose the Edit Macro command.

   You see a submenu of choices.

2. Choose the Run Macro command.

   You see the Run Macro dialog box (see fig. 12.11). Here you select the macro you want to run.

Figure 12.11. The Run Macro dialog box.

3. In the Macros, list click on the name of the macro you want to run.

   You can click on the scroll arrows to scroll through the list.

4. Choose the Run button.

ACT! carries out the steps you recorded.

If the macro didn't work as you expected, you need to find out where the problem occurred. Run the macro again, but this time display the Playback Speed drop-down list in the Run Macro dialog box. Select At Recorded Speed and then choose Run. ACT! plays back the macro steps at the speed these steps were recorded. At this slower speed, you should be able to spot the problem. After you find the problem, make a note of it and rerecord the macro.

TIP: *If you use a macro often, add it to an icon. See the following section.*

Adding a Macro to the Icon Bar

You can add a macro to an icon on the icon bar so that the macro is easily accessible. Follow these steps:

1. Choose the Edit Preferences command.

   You see the Preferences dialog box.

2. Choose the Custom Icons option.

   You see a list of Custom Icons options (see fig. 12.12). The installed icons are listed on the top right half of the dialog box. Additional icons appear below.

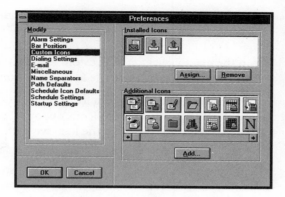

Figure 12.12. Adding a macro to an icon.

3. If the icon you want to use appears in the Installed Icons area, click on it and then click the Assign button. If the icon doesn't appear in the area, click on another icon in the Additional Icons area and click the Add button.

   You can use the scroll arrows to scroll through the additional icons. Both of these actions display the Choose Macro dialog box (see fig. 12.13). You see a list of macros.

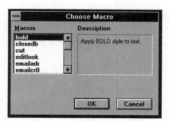

Figure 12.13. The Choose Macro dialog box.

4. Click on the macro name in the Macros list.

   If you can't remember the name, use the Description text to help you find the macro that you want to add. You can assign macros you created, or you can assign the built-in macros provided with ACT!

5. Choose the OK button.

   You are returned to the Preferences dialog box.

6. To close the dialog box, choose OK.

The icon is added to the icon bar. The following checklist summarizes how to use, change, or remove the custom icon:

✔ To run the macro, click on the custom icon. ACT! runs the macro just as if you had selected it using the Edit Macro Run Macro command.

✔ If you want to delete the custom icon, choose the Edit Preferences command. Choose the Custom Icons option. Click on the icon you want to remove and then click the Remove button.

✔ To change what macro is assigned to a button, choose the Edit Preferences command and then choose the Custom Icons option. Click the icon you want to change. Then click the Assign button. Select the macro you want. Choose OK twice.

Deleting a Macro

If you no longer need a macro, you can delete it. The macro is stored as a file with the extension MAC. Follow these steps to delete the macro:

1. Choose the Edit Macro command.

   You see a submenu of choices.

2. Choose the Delete Macro command.

   You see the Delete Macro dialog box.

3. In the Macros list, click on the macro you want to delete.

   You can use the scroll arrows to scroll through the list.

4. Choose the Delete button.

   You are asked to confirm the deletion.

5. Choose the Yes button.

The macro is deleted.

Using a Description File

When you customize the database—create user fields, change field defaults—the new customized format is saved with the database file. You also can save the customized information—stored in a description file—and attach this file to other databases.

Table 12.2 lists the description files provided with ACT!.

Table 12.2. ACT! Description Files

File Name	Description
BUSINESS	Fields for business use, including Annual Billing, Client Class, Service Frequency, Service Rate, Contact Class, Prtnr Assigned, Now Retain, Reason Retain, and Special Needs.
COMMRE	For commercial real estate. Includes fields for Map Coordinate, Class/Zone, Square Ft., Fin/Unfin, Occupancy, Special Needs, Expenses, Price/SqFt., # Locations, Commission, Mth/Close, Competitor, SIC, and Lease Expire.
INSURANC	For insurance sales. Includes fields for Age, Dependents, Birthdate, Customer Since, Reason, Interest Area, Coverage Now, Proposed Type, Dollar Value.
MANAGER	For sales managers. Includes fields for Next Objective, Last Order $, YTD Revenue, Business Class, Contact Class, Credit Status, Hotbuttons, Memberships, and Reminder.
PROJLDR	Useful for project leaders. Includes fields for Start Date, Due Date, Probable Date, Dept. Assigned, Group Leader, and Expertise.
RESRE	Useful for residential real estate agents. Includes fields for Price, Bed/Bth/Garage, Living, Dining, Map Coord, Legal Description, Amenities, Bonus, Expense, Commission Rate, Lot, Reduction, Contract, and Close Date.
DEFAULT	Use this file if you edit the fields and want to return to the default field names and types.

TIP: *ACT! also provides several description files that you can review to get ideas for your database.*

Saving a Description File

To save a description file, follow these steps:

1. Choose the File Database Settings command.

   You see the Database Settings dialog box (see fig. 12.14).

Figure 12.14. The Database Settings dialog box.

    2. Choose the Save As button.

       You see the Save Description File dialog box. Here you enter a name for the file. ACT! automatically assigns the DES extension and by default stores the file in the C:\ACTWIN2\DATABASE directory.

    3. Type a file name and choose OK.

The description file is saved. To attach the description file to another database, see the next section.

Attaching a Description File

When you want to use the description file on another database, start by opening the database you want to change. Then follow these steps:

    1. Choose the File Database Settings command.

       You see the Database Settings dialog box.

    2. Choose the Apply button.

       You see the Apply Description File dialog box (see fig. 12.15).

    3. In the File Name list, click on the description file and choose OK.

ACT! updates the current database and displays the user defined fields for the description file. Figure 12.15 and 12.16 show the contact screens with COMMRE description file applied to the DEMO database.

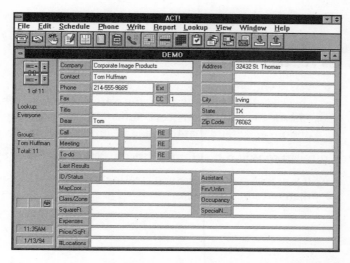

Figure 12.15. The first contact screen, using the COMMRE description file.

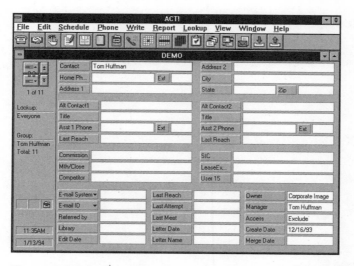

Figure 12.16. The second contact screen using the COMMRE description file.

Q&A

I thought I set alarms, but I am never reminded about calls or meetings. How can I fix this?

✔ When you create an activity be sure that the Set Alarm check box is checked. Also, make sure that the alarms have not been disabled. Choose the Edit Preferences command and choose the Alarm Settings option. Make sure that there is an X in the Enable Alarm check box.

I made a mistake when creating a macro. What do I do now?

✔ If you make a mistake when creating a macro, delete the original and then rerecord the macro.

Maintaining the Database

Maintaining the database isn't a daily task, but it should not be ignored. Your contact database includes vital information that should be backed up to be kept secure. You also need to weed out old contacts so that your database isn't overloaded with unnecessary information.

This chapter covers these key database maintenance tasks:

- Backing up the database
- Purging notes and histories
- Purging contacts
- Deleting a document
- Using passwords

Time-Management Tip

Consider separating your filing into the following categories: completed work you need to file, tasks you need to do now (bills, reports, letters, and so on), information you need to read, and information that you need to pass on to others.

Backing Up the Database

The information in your database is the key to your success. If something happens to the information, it may take hours, days, or weeks to re-enter it, and some of it may be irreplaceable. This is why periodically backing up your database is a good idea—you'll have an extra copy in case something happens to the original.

ACT! doesn't provide a backup command, so you need to use a manual procedure to back up the database. You can use any of the following strategies.

Using File Save As

If the database is small, you can use the File Save As command to save a copy of your database to a disk. You may want to use this command if you need to give a group of contacts to a colleague. For example, suppose that your sales territory has grown too large, and you are going to turn over all contacts in certain states to another representative. You can copy the database by using the File Save As command.

> **NOTE:** *The File Save As command won't work if the database is too large. In this case, the disk cannot hold all the necessary database files, and you need to try another backup procedure.*

To save a copy of your database by using the File Save As command, follow these steps:

1. If you want to save only some contacts, create a lookup group for the contacts you want.

   ACT! enables you to save the active contact, the active lookup, or all contacts.

2. Choose the File Save As command.

   You are prompted to select the records you want to include (see fig. 13.1).

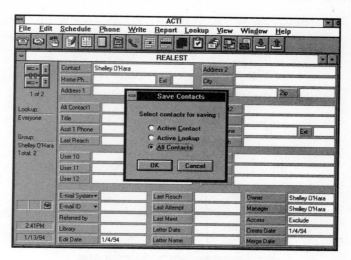

Figure 13.1. Using the File Save As command.

3. Select the contacts to include and choose OK.

   You see the Save Database As dialog box (see fig. 13.2).

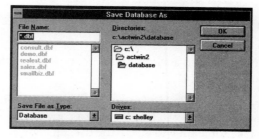

Figure 13.2. Saving the database to another drive.

4. Display the Drives drop-down list and choose drive A or B.

   The drive you select depends on which drive you inserted the backup disk into. If you inserted the disk in drive A (usually the top drive), choose A. If you inserted the disk in drive B, choose B.

5. Choose OK.

   You are prompted to confirm the information in "My Record."

6. Make any changes and choose OK.

   You are asked to confirm whether the information is correct.

7. Choose Yes.

   You are prompted to type a password for the new database (see fig. 13.3).

Figure 13.3. Typing a password.

8. If you want to assign a password, type it and choose OK. Otherwise, just choose OK.

See the section on "Using Passwords" for more information on creating and changing passwords. ACT! will create a copy of the file on the selected drive. It may take some time to create the backup copy.

To use the backup copy, copy the files on the disk to the C:\ACTWIN2\DATABASE directory and then use the File Open command. You also can use the File Open command and open the file on the disk, but working from a disk can be very slow.

Copying the Files Manually

If your database is too large and you don't know how to or don't like to use a backup program (described next), you can manually copy the files to another drive. Use the File Manager provided with Windows. The benefit of this program is that if the file(s) is too large to fit on one disk, the File Manager will prompt you to insert another disk. Large files can be stored this way across several disks. When they are reloaded onto a computer, the files will automatically be put back together.

ACT! stores different file types in different directories. Table 13.1 lists the file types and ACT! directories.

Table 13.1. ACT! Directory Organization

File Type	Directory Name
Briefcase	C:\ACTWIN2\BCASE
Database	C:\ACTWIN2\DATABASE
Deferred print jobs	C:\ACTWIN2\DEFERRED
Documents	C:\ACTWIN2\DOCS
Filters for import and export	C:\ACTWIN2\FILTERS
Layouts	C:\ACTWIN2\LAYOUTS
Macros	C:\ACTWIN2\MACROS
Mail	C:\ACTWIN2\MAIL
Outbox mail	C:\ACTWIN2\OUTBOX
Printouts	C:\ACTWIN2\PRINTOUT
Queries	C:\ACTWIN2\QUERIES
Reports	C:\ACTWIN2\REPORTS
Spell	C:\ACTWIN2\SPELL
Templates	C:\ACTWIN2\TEMPLATE

The most critical files to back up are the database files. Follow these steps to use the File Manager to copy the database files:

1. From the Program Manager, open the Main program group.

    This is the program group that houses the File Manager icon.

2. Double-click the File Manager icon.

   The File Manager is displayed on-screen.

3. Double-click on the ACTWIN2 directory.

   You see the subdirectories within this directory.

4. Click on the DATABASE directory.

   You see the database files listed on the right side of the File Manager window (see fig. 13.4). An ACT! contact database consists of files with the following extensions: ADB, ADX, DBF, DES, EDB, FPT, GRP, GRX, HDB, HDX, MDX, MUD, NDB, and NDX. The files for one database are listed next to each other because the files have the same root name. For instance, the files for the SALES database would be SALES.ADB, SALES.ADX, etc. In this example, SALES is the root name, so you would select all files beginning with SALES.

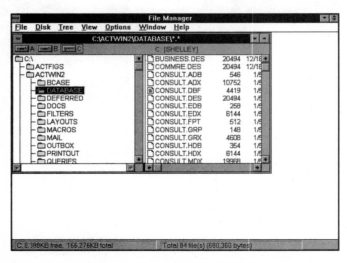

Figure 13.4. The files in the DATABASE directory.

5. Click on the first file in the group. Press and hold down the Shift key and click on the last file in the group.

   This step selects all files between and including the first and last file. These are the files you want to copy.

6. Choose the File Copy command.

   You see the Copy dialog box (see fig. 13.5).

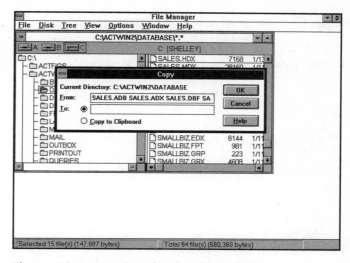

Figure 13.5. Copying the database files.

7. In the To text box, type A: or B:.

   If you are copying the files to drive A, type A:. To copy the files to drive B, type B:. Don't forget to type the colon.

8. Choose OK.

ACT! copies the selected files to the disk. If all the files won't fit on one disk, you are prompted to insert additional disks. Follow the on-screen prompts.

If something happens to your original files, you can copy the files from the disks back to the C:\ACTWIN2\DATABASE directory.

NOTE: *To use DOS to copy the database files, type the following command, and then press Enter:*

COPY C:\ACTWIN2\DATABASE\.* A:

For filename, *type the name of your database file. For example, if your database is named* sales, *type SALES.*.*

Using a Backup Command or Program

You also can use the DOS BACKUP command to backup files or, if you have another backup program, you can use it to backup your key files.

To backup all ACT! files, including the program files, use the following DOS command:

C:\BACKUP C:\ACTWIN2*.* /S A:

This command tells DOS to back up all files (*.*) and all subdirectories (/S) in the ACTWIN2 directory to drive A.

DOS Version 6 includes a backup program called MSBACKUP. If you have this program or another backup program, follow the instructions for that program to backup ACT! files.

Purging Notes and Histories

As your database becomes larger and larger, you will want to periodically purge the notes and histories. The notes and history information take up disk space and can slow down the performance of ACT!. You can purge the notes and/or histories for all contacts or a group of contacts. You also can select a date range to purge.

Follow these steps:

1. Choose the File Maintenance command.

   You see the Maintenance dialog box (see fig. 13.6).

Figure 13.6. The Maintenance dialog box.

2. Check with items you want to purge: Purge Notes, Purge History.

    You can select one or both options, depending on what you want to purge.

3. Choose OK.

    You see an on-screen calendar (see fig. 13.7).

Figure 13.7. Selecting a date range.

4. Drag across the range you want to purge. If you want to purge all dates, choose the All Dates button. To purge all past dates, choose the Past button.

ACT! purges the notes or histories from the database. You see a status bar that displays the progress of the purge.

Purging Contacts

As you add more and more contacts, you may find that some contacts are unnecessary. Perhaps a different person took over that person's job, and you no longer need the original contacts record. Or perhaps you are turning over some contacts to another sales representative. To help your database run as efficiently as possible, you can get rid of contacts you no longer need and reindex the database.

Time-Management Tip

Develop and use a good filing system. A good filing system will help you avoid looking all over for something you need. Also, a good filing system will keep your desk or office uncluttered.

Deleting a Group of Contacts

You can delete contacts one by one, as described in Chapter 2, "Setting Up a Contact Database." This would be time-consuming if you wanted to delete an entire group of contacts. To delete a group more simply, create a lookup group for the contacts you want to delete. For instance, suppose that you are no longer in charge of sales in Indiana. You can group all contacts for IN and delete them.

CAUTION: *Before you delete a group of contacts, backup the group or the entire database. If you accidentally delete the wrong contacts or if you need them at a later date, you can use the backup copy.*

Follow these steps to delete a group of contacts:

1. Display the group on-screen.

    Create a lookup group to display the records you want. Lookups are covered in Chapter 3, "Managing Contacts."

2. Choose the Edit Delete Contact command.

    You see the Delete Contact dialog box (see fig. 13.8).

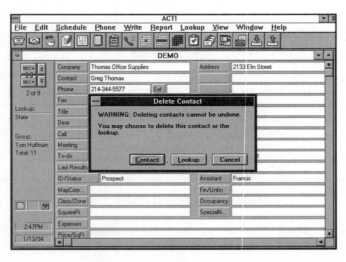

Figure 13.8. Deleting a group of contacts.

3. Choose Lookup.

    You are asked to confirm that you want to delete all contacts in the current lookup.

4. Choose Yes.

    You are asked whether you want to delete the last contact with the lookups.

5. Choose Yes.

ACT! deletes the contacts from the database. To regain the disk space and performance, you need to compress and reindex, as described in the next section.

Reindexing and Compressing the Database

ACT! keeps track of records using several different files. The index files, for instance, help ACT! quickly find a record. When you delete records, you should reindex the database. You should also compress the database to regain the disk space that was used by the deleted contacts.

Follow these steps:

1. Choose the File Maintenance command.

    You see the Maintenance dialog box.

2. Choose the Compress and reindex database option if you have deleted a substantial number of contacts. This option will compress the index and takes longer than just reindexing. Otherwise, choose the Reindex database command.

3. Choose OK.

You see progress bars on-screen as ACT! performs the necessary steps to compress and reindex the database.

CAUTION: *Don't interrupt the compress and reindex process. Doing so can damage the current database.*

Deleting a Document

If you need to delete a file—for instance, documents that you no longer need—you can use the File Delete command. You should periodically clean up your hard disk and get rid of files you don't need. Doing so frees space for other more important files.

Follow these steps to delete a document:

1. Choose the File Delete command.

   You see the Delete File dialog box (see fig. 13.9). If you choose this command from the contact screen, you see database files listed. If you choose this command from the word processor, word processing files are listed. You can change the type of file that is displayed.

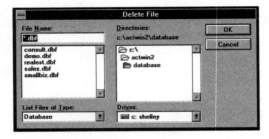

Figure 13.9. Deleting a file.

2. If necessary, display the List Files of Type drop-down list and select the type of file you want to delete.

   For instance, choose Document to list WPD or word processing files.

3. In the file list, click on the file you want to delete.

   You can use the scroll bars to scroll through the list and find the file you want.

4. Choose OK.

   ACT! displays an alert box asking you to confirm the deletion.

5. Choose Yes to delete the file.

The file is deleted.

Time-Management Tip

Handle paper only once. Decide immediately what to do with it: throw it out, act on it, pass it along, file it.

Using Passwords

When you create a new database, you can assign a password. If you want to change the password or if you did not add one and want to now, you can do so.

CAUTION: *Write down your password and keep the note locked away in your safe. If you forget your password, you won't be able to access the database.*

Follow these steps:

1. Choose the File Database Settings command.

   You see the Database Settings dialog box.

2. Choose the Password button.

   ACT! displays the Change Password dialog box (see fig. 13.10).

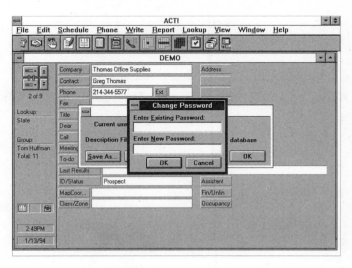

Figure 13.10. Adding or changing a password.

3. If you are changing the password, type the original password, press Tab, and type the new password. If you are adding a password, press Tab and type the new password. Choose OK.

You are prompted to confirm the password.

4. Type the password again and choose OK.

ACT! assigns the password to the database and closes the Change Password dialog box.

5. Choose OK.

This step closes the Database Settings dialog box.

The next time you open this database, you will be prompted to type the password (see fig. 13.11). Type the password and choose OK.

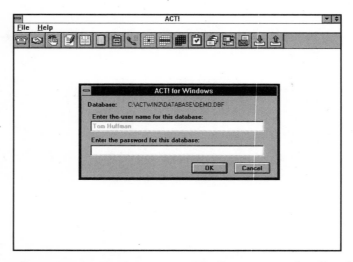

Figure 13.11. Typing a password to open a database file.

Q&A

Can I undelete a file?

✓ You cannot undelete a file while you use ACT! You can, however, use the DOS UNDELETE command to undelete a file. You must have DOS version 5 or 6. Some third-party utility programs, such as the Norton Utilities and PC Tools, also provide tools that enable you to delete a file.

For specific instructions on how to undelete a file, see your DOS manual or utility program manual.

I get an error message when I try to delete a file. Why?

✓ You cannot delete a document you currently have open. Close the document, and then try deleting the file.

Appendixes

Installing ACT!

This appendix explains how to install the ACT! program. Information on setting up a printer and modem are also included.

Running the Install Program

Before you can use ACT!, you need to run the Install program. The Install program creates directories for different file types, copies the necessary files to your hard disk, and adds a new program group and program icons. Follow these steps:

1. From the Windows Program Manager, choose the File Run command.

   You see the Run dialog box.

2. Insert the first program disk in drive A or B and type A:\INSTALL or B:\INSTALL.

   Figure A.1 shows the command you type to run the install program.

Figure A.1. The Run dialog box.

3. Choose OK.

   You see the ACT! 2.0 for Windows dialog box (see fig. A.2).

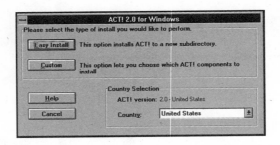

Figure A.2. In this dialog box, select the type of install you want.

4. To install all program components, choose Easy Install and skip to step 6. To select which components are installed, choose Custom.

You see the Custom Install dialog box (see fig. A.3).

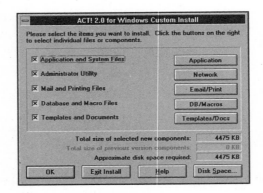

Figure A.3. The Custom Install dialog box.

5. Check the main components you want to install. To select individual components, click the button next to the main component. Check the individual items you want installed. Then choose OK.

You are prompted to select the directory and drive on which to install ACT! (see fig. A.4). The default drive is C, and the default directory is C:\ACTWIN2.

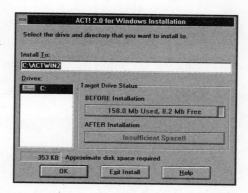

Figure A.4. Selecting the drive and directory for ACT!

6. If you want to select another directory, type the new directory name in the Install To text box. If you have more than one hard drive and want to install the program on a drive other than C, select the drive in the Drives list. Choose OK.

   ACT! begins copying the needed files to the disk. You see a progress bar on-screen. You are prompted to insert the second disk (see fig. A.5).

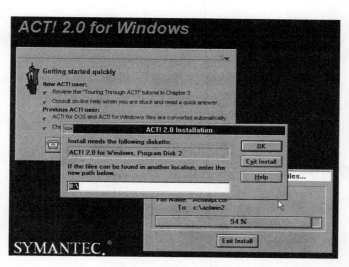

Figure A.5. You are prompted to insert the second disk.

7. Insert the next disk and choose OK.

    Next you see the registration form.

8. Complete the requested information and choose OK.

    Figure A.6 shows a completed form.

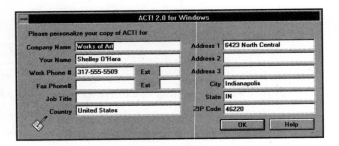

Figure A.6. The on-screen registration.

You are prompted to confirm the information.

9. Choose Yes if the information is correct. Otherwise, choose No, make corrections, choose OK, and then choose Yes.

    You are asked to select a method for processing the form.

10. Choose Modem to send the registration form by modem. Choose Print to print the form. Choose Cancel to skip printing.

    You see a message stating that ACT! was successfully installed.

11. Choose OK.

    You are returned to the Program Manager.

Importing Your Database

If you used version 1 or 1.1 of ACT! for Windows, you can open your database by using the File Open command. ACT! opens and converts all your records. To import data from a different ACT! version or from another program, see Appendix B.

Setting Up Your Printer

To use a printer with ACT!, you set up and install the printer by using Windows. See your Windows manual for information on installing printers. If you have more than one printer installed, you can switch between them.

For example, if you have a FAX/modem, you have a printer driver for the FAX/Modem. (Basically, you print to the modem.) You also can set printer options.

To set up the printer, follow these steps:

1. Choose the File Printer Setup command.

   Note that this command is available only when you are in a word processing window. If necessary, open or create a word processing document. You see the Print Setup dialog box (see fig. A.7).

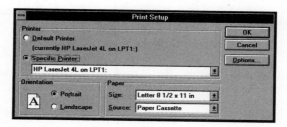

Figure A.7. The Print Setup dialog box.

2. To choose the printer that you want to use, display the Specific Printer drop-down list and click on the name of the desired printer.

   ACT! lists the printers that you have installed using the Windows Control Panel.

3. If you want to, choose an orientation: Portrait or Landscape.

   The default is portrait.

4. To change the paper size or source, display the Size drop-down list or the Source drop-down list and choose the size and source you want.

   For example, if your printer can print on legal-size paper, you can select this paper option from the Size list. Some printers have a manual feed and a bin. You can select which method to use as the source. On some printers, you have to feed envelopes manually.

5. To change the printer options, choose the Options button.

   You see the Options dialog box. The options you see depend on the printer you have. Figure A.8 shows the options for an HP LaserJet 4L.

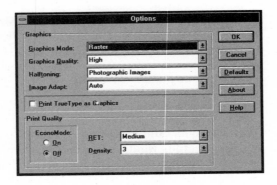

Figure A.8. Printer options for the HP LaserJet 4L.

6. Select the options you want.

   You may have options for the graphics mode, quality, and so on.

7. Choose OK.

   You are returned to the Printer Setup dialog box.

8. Choose OK.

You are returned to the document. The next time you print, ACT! uses the printer and options you selected.

Setting Up Your Modem

If you have a modem installed on your computer, you can use ACT! to make phone calls and to send data. Follow these steps to set up your modem:

1. Choose the Edit Preferences command.

   You see the Preferences dialog box.

2. Choose Dialing Settings.

   You see the Dialing Settings options (see fig. A.9).

3. If you need to change the initialize command, type the command used to initialize the modem in the Initialize text box.

   The default command is the Hayes command. Most modems are Hayes compatible. Check your modem manual for information on the command you need if your modem is not Hayes compatible.

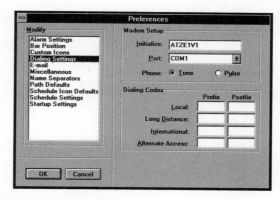

Figure A.9. The Dialing Settings.

4. Display the Port drop-down list and choose the port.

   Choose the port to which your modem is attached. Modems are usually attached to COM1 or COM2.

5. Select the type of phone you have—Tone or Pulse.

   If you have touch buttons and hear musical notes when you dial, use tone. If you have a rotary dial and hear clicks when you dial, use pulse.

6. In the Dialing Codes area, enter any dialing codes necessary to dial out.

   For example, if you must dial a 9 to gain access to an outside line, enter 9 in the Prefix boxes. If you must dial a 1 for long distance, enter a 1 in the Prefix for Long Distance.

7. Choose OK.

   The modem is set up.

Importing and Exporting Data

If your contact information is in another format, you can *import* the data from that program to ACT!. Importing reads information from another file type and makes the data fit ACT!s format.

If you need to share data with someone who doesn't have ACT!, you can *export* the data. Exporting the data saves ACT! data in a format that another program can read, such as dBASE. You also can transfer data from one database to another or merge data from one database with another. This appendix discusses these import and export tasks.

Importing Data

If you want to use data in another format, you import it. You can import the following database files:

File Type	Description
CCD, CCX	Previous versions of ACT! database files (ACT! for DOS 2.0 and 2.1, 1stACT for DOS)
TXT	Delimited files
DBF	dBASE III or IV files
DTF	Q&A Data files

> **TIP:** *If you are importing data from another program not listed in the preceding list, you may have to take an in between step. Most programs can save files in a delimited (TXT) format. In the original file, save the database by using this format, and then, using the following steps, import the database.*

To import a database file, follow these steps:

1. Choose the File Import/Exchange command.

   You see a submenu of choices.

2. Choose the Import command.

   You see the Import File dialog box (see fig. B.1).

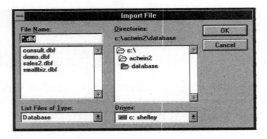

Figure B.1. The Import File dialog box.

TIP: *Press Alt+F12 to choose the File Import/Exchange command.*

---

3. Display the List Files of Type drop-down list and select the file type.

   The file type you select should match the file type of the original file. For example, if you are importing a dBASE file, select dBASE as the file type.

   ACT! lists files that match the type selected.

4. If necessary, change to the drive or directory that contains the file.

ACT! displays files in the C:\ACTWIN2\DATABASE directory. If the file you want to import is in another directory, double-click on it in the Directories list. If the file is on another drive, display the Drive's drop-down list and select the drive.

5. When the file you want is displayed, click on it in the File Name list and then click OK.

   You also can double-click on the file name as a shortcut. For ACT! files, ACT! converts and adds the records to the current database. You are finished.

For delimited and dBASE files, ACT! displays the Importing Options dialog box (see fig. B.2). Using this dialog box, you tell ACT! how the data matches the ACT! fields.

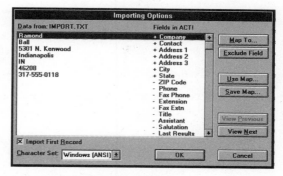

Figure B.2. The Importing Options dialog box.

The data from the file is listed in the first column. The fields in ACT! are listed in the second column.

If the first record contains field names rather than data, you can exclude this record by unchecking the Import First Record check box.

6. To map a data entry to its correct field, click on the data, and then click on the Map To button.

You see the Map Fields dialog box (see fig. B.3).

Figure B.3. The Map Fields dialog box.

7. Click on the correct field name and choose OK.

You can use the scroll arrows to scroll through the list and find the appropriate field.

> **TIP:** *If the original database included separate fields for first and last name, don't map the names to the Contact field. Instead, map the first name to the First Name field and the last name to the Last Name field.*

8. Follow steps 6 and 7 for all fields in the original database.

    To exclude a field from the database, click on the data item and click the Exclude Field button.

9. To view other records and be sure they are matched correctly, click the View Next button. To view previous records, click the View Previous button.

    When you are sure all the fields are mapped correctly, go on to the next step.

> **TIP:** *If you are going to import other files set up in this format, save the map file so that you don't have to manually match data and fields again. Click the Save Map button. Then type a file name and choose OK. When you want to use the map file again, click the Use Map button, select the file name, and choose OK.*

10. Choose OK.

    You are prompted to confirm that the import options are set correctly.

11. Choose OK if the options are correct. Otherwise, choose Cancel and make any corrections.

    ACT! imports and adds the records to the current database.

Exporting Data

If you need to use the information in your database in another program, you can save the database in another format. You can export both database and document files.

Exporting a Database File

You can save the database in a previous version of ACT! file type or in a delimited file. Most other programs can work with delimited files. Follow these steps:

1. Open the database that you want to export. If you want to export just a group of records, create a lookup group. If you want to export just one record, display that record.

    Opening, finding, and looking up groups of records are covered in Chapter 3, "Managing Contacts."

2. Choose the File Save As command.

    You are prompted to select which contacts to save (see fig. B.4).

Figure B.4. The Save Contacts dialog box.

3. Select which contacts to save: Active Contact, Active Lookup, All Contacts. Then choose OK.

    ACT! displays the Save Database As dialog box (see fig. B.5).

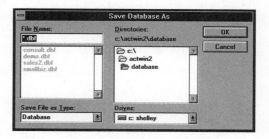

Figure B.5. The Save Database As dialog box.

4. Display the Save File as Type drop-down list and select the file type you want.

    For example, to save the file as a delimited file, choose Delimited.

5. Type a file name and choose OK.

    If you choose Delimited, ACT! displays the Exporting Options dialog box (see fig. B.6).

Figure B.6. The Exporting Options dialog box.

6. Choose a delimiter: Comma or Tab.

   A delimiter is what is used to separate the fields from each other. Check the program you are exporting to find the delimiter you need.

7. If you want to export the user fields, check the Export Secondary Fields check box. If you want to export the field names, check the Export Field Names check box.

ACT! exports the data to the new file.

Exporting a Document File

If you create a word processing file that you want to use in another program, you can save it as another file type. Follow these steps:

1. Open the word processing file you want to save.

   Chapters 8 and 9 cover creating and formatting word processing documents.

2. Choose the File Save As command.

   ACT! displays the Save As dialog box (see fig. B.7).

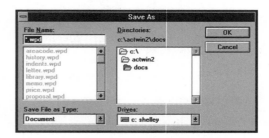

Figure B.7. The Save As dialog box.

3. Display the Save File as Type drop-down list and select the file type you want.

   You can choose RTF or Text. Most word processing programs accept both file types.

4. Type a file name and choose OK.

ACT! saves the file in the new format.

Transferring Data to Another Database

If you work with more than one database, you can transfer records among the databases. For example, you may initially set up one database with all your contacts. As time goes on, you may have several hundred contacts and may want to separate them by type—for example, put all personal contacts in one database and all business in another. You can transfer data from one database to another.

To transfer data, follow these steps:

1. If necessary, create and save the database to which you want to transfer records.

   If you already created the database, you can skip this step. If you are separating records into two or more databases, create the new database(s).

2. Open the database from which you want to transfer the records.

   This database contains the records you want to transfer. You can transfer the current record, all records in the active lookup, or all records.

3. To transfer an individual record, display the record. To transfer just a group of records, create a lookup group to group the records you want.

   Chapter 3 covers lookups in detail.

4. Choose the File Import/Exchange command.

   You see a submenu.

5. Choose the Transfer command.

   You see the Transfer Contacts dialog box (see fig. B.8).

Figure B.8. The Transfer Contacts dialog box.

6. Select which records you want transferred: Active Contact, Active Lookup, All Contacts. Then choose OK. You see the Transfer Contacts To dialog box (see fig. B.9).

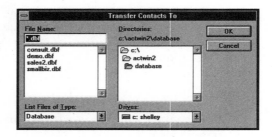

Figure B.9. The Transfer Contacts To dialog box.

7. Select the database to which you want to transfer the records and then choose OK.

   ACT! transfers the records to the database and asks whether you want to delete the contact(s) from the original database.

8. Choose Yes to delete the contact, choose No to keep the contact.

If you choose Yes, you are asked to confirm the deletion, and you also are asked whether you want the last contact deleted. You are then returned to the contact screen.

Merging Data

If needed, you can combine contacts—that is, merge contacts from one database to another. The database that will contain the merged records is the *destination* database. The database that contains the records you want to merge is the *source* database. Follow these steps to merge the two:

1. Open the destination database.

   Remember, this is the database that will contain the merged and original records.

2. Choose the File Import/Exchange command.

   You see a submenu of choices.

3. Choose the Merge command.

   You see the Merge Source File dialog box (see fig. B.10).

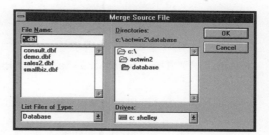

Figure B.10. The Merge Source File dialog box.

4. Click the file name and choose OK.

   This source file contains the records you want to merge. You see the Merge dialog box (see fig. B.11).

Figure B.11. The Merge dialog box.

5. To change any of the merge settings, click the Custom button.

   You see the Customize Merge dialog box (see fig. B.12).

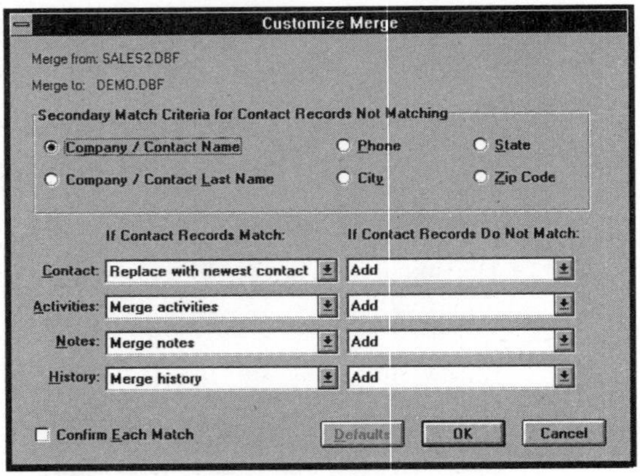

Figure B.12. The Customize Merge dialog box.

6. Choose the field that you want to match:

   Company/Contact Name

   Company/Last Name

   Phone

   City

   State

   Zip Code

7. Choose how you want the contact records handled:

   For contacts that match, display the Contact drop-down list and choose to replace the contact with the newest record, replace the contact with the source contact, or do not change. To determine the newest record, compare the last editing dates. For contacts that do not match, choose whether you want to add the contact.

8. Choose how you want the activities handled:

   For contacts that match, display the Activities drop-down list and choose to merge the activities, replace with source activities, or do not change. For contacts that don't match, choose whether you want to add the activities.

9. Choose how you want the notes handled:

   For contacts that match, display the Notes drop-down list and choose to merge the notes, replace with source notes, or do not change. For contacts that don't match, choose whether you want to add the notes.

10. Choose how you want the history handled:

    For contacts that match, display the History drop-down list and choose to merge the history or do not change. For contacts that do not match, choose whether you want to add the history.

11. If you want to confirm each match, check the Confirm Each Match check box.

    By default, ACT! doesn't ask you to confirm each match.

12. Choose OK.

    The Customize Merge dialog box is closed, and you are returned to the Merge dialog box.

13. Choose the Merge button.

    ACT! merges the records. If you check the Confirm Each Match, you are prompted to merge the record or skip the record.

Linking to a HP 95LX Palmtop

If you have a HP 95LX palmtop PC, you can link the palmtop and desktop computers. You must first connect the cables. See your HP manual for information on hooking up the cables. You can both send and receive data.

Sending Data

To send data from the desktop to the palmtop, follow these steps:

1. Open the database that contains the records you want to link. If you want to transfer a group of records, create a lookup group.

   For information on lookup groups, see Chapter 3.

2. Choose the File Import/Exchange command.

   You see a submenu of choices.

3. Choose the Direct Link command.

   You see the Direct Link Settings dialog box.

4. Choose the Send to device option and select the appropriate COM port. Then choose OK.

   You see the Transfer Contacts dialog box.

5. Choose which contacts you want transferred: Active Contact, Active Lookup, All Contacts. Then choose OK.

You see the Direct Link Data dialog box.

6. Display the Contact drop-down list and choose which contact data to send: Copy all fields or Copy basic fields only.

   Basic fields include the Company, Contact, Title, Phone, Extension, Country Code, Dear, Sec, Address 1-3, City, State, Zip, ID/Status, Owner, Manager, and Alternate Phone, Extension, Address 1-2, City, State, and Zip.

7. Display the History drop-down list and choose the entries that you want to send: Copy all entries, Copy 2, 4, or 8 latest entries, or None.

8. Display the Notes drop-down list and choose which entries to send: Copy all entries, Copy 2, 4, or 8 latest entries, or None.

9. Display the Activities drop-down list and choose which entries to send: Copy all entries, Copy 2, 4, or 8 latest entries, or None.

10. Select the descriptions to use—PC or HP.

11. Choose OK.

ACT! sends the information from the desktop and sends the selected data to the palmtop PC.

Receiving Data

To receive data from the palmtop, follow these steps:

1. Open the database that contains the database you want to receive the information.

2. Choose the File Import/Exchange command.

   You see a submenu of choices.

3. Choose the Direct Link command.

   You see the Direct Link Settings dialog box.

4. Choose the Receive from device option and select the appropriate COM port. Then choose OK.

   You see the Select Contacts for Merge dialog box.

5. Choose which contacts you want:

Option	Description
All Edited Contacts	Merges all new and edited contacts from the palmtop to the desktop PC.
Last Edited Date Range	Displays a calendar. Drag across the dates you want to include. ACT! will merge all new or edited contacts within the selected date range.

You see the Merge dialog box.

6. Choose which field you want to match:

   Company/Contact Name

   Company/Last Name

   Phone

   City

   State

   Zip Code

7. Choose how you want the contact records handled:

   For contacts that match, display the Contact drop-down list and choose to replace the contact with the newest record, replace the contact with the source contact, or do not change. To determine the newest record, compare the last editing dates. For contacts that do not match, choose whether to add the contact.

8. Choose how you want the activities handled:

   For contacts that match, display the Activities drop-down list and choose to merge the activities, replace with source activities, or do not change. For contacts that do not match, choose whether to add the activities.

9. Choose how you want the notes handled:

   For contacts that match, display the Notes drop-down list and choose to merge the notes, replace with source notes, or do not change. For contacts that do not match, choose whether to add the notes.

10. Choose how you want the history handled:

    For contacts that match, display the History drop-down list and choose to merge the history or don't change. For contacts that do not match, choose whether to add the history.

11. If you want to confirm each match, check the Confirm Each Match check box.

    By default, ACT! does not ask you to confirm each match.

12. Choose OK.

    The Customize Merge dialog box is closed, and you are returned to the Merge dialog box.

13. Choose the Merge button.

    ACT! merges the records. If you check the Confirm Each Match, you are prompted to merge the record or skip the record.

Index

Symbols

* (asterisk) wild card, 58
<< button, help system, 20
>> button, help system, 20
0-9 data type, 41

A

ACT!
 exiting, 22
 for small businesses,
 81-84
 installing, 273-276
 starting, 11-13, 13
ACT! 2.0 for Windows
 dialog box, 273-274
ACT! Printouts dialog box,
 73-77, 120-124
ACT! program group/icon
 finding, 22
 opening, 12-13
activities
 clearing, 104-105
 lookups by priority,
 115-116
 scheduling, 102-106
 task list, 112-115

Timeless, 118
 timing, 100-101
 total, viewing, 112
 tracking, 125
Activities Completed report
 format, 148
activity lists, 110-111
Add button, 40
Add Custom Menu Item
 dialog box, 63, 166,
 229-230
Add E-Mail Address dialog
 box, 128-129
Address Book Options
 dialog box, 74-76
address books, printing,
 73-77
addresses (e-mail), 128-129
alarms
 preferences, 236-237
 responding to, 99-100
 setting, 254
aligning text, 200-201
Alt+key letter, selecting
 commands, 15
AND Boolean operator, 60
AND NOT Boolean opera-
 tor, 61

Apply Description File
 dialog box, 252
arrow keys, 172
asterisk (*) wild card, 58
attaching
 description files, 252-253
 files/contacts to e-mail
 messages, 132-134
attributes (fields), 40-42
automatic popup menus, 41
automatic dialing, 93-95,
 106
Avery labels, 225-226

B

Back button, help system, 20
backing up databases,
 255-256
 copying manually,
 259-261
 DOS commands for, 262
 saving with new names,
 256-258
Backspace key, 171
BACKUP command, 262
bar positions preferences,
 237-238

GO AHEAD. PLUG YOURSELF INTO
PRENTICE HALL COMPUTER PUBLISHING.

Introducing the PHCP Forum on CompuServe®

Yes, it's true. Now, you can have CompuServe access to the same professional, friendly folks who have made computers easier for years. On the PHCP Forum, you'll find additional information on the topics covered by every PHCP imprint—including Que, Sams Publishing, New Riders Publishing, Alpha Books, Brady Books, Hayden Books, and Adobe Press. In addition, you'll be able to receive technical support and disk updates for the software produced by Que Software and Paramount Interactive, a division of the Paramount Technology Group. It's a great way to supplement the best information in the business.

WHAT CAN YOU DO ON THE PHCP FORUM?

Play an important role in the publishing process—and make our books better while you make your work easier:

■ Leave messages and ask questions about PHCP books and software—you're guaranteed a response within 24 hours

■ Download helpful tips and software to help you get the most out of your computer

■ Contact authors of your favorite PHCP books through electronic mail

■ Present your own book ideas

■ Keep up to date on all the latest books available from each of PHCP's exciting imprints

JOIN NOW AND GET A FREE COMPUSERVE STARTER KIT!

To receive your free CompuServe Introductory Membership, call toll-free, **1-800-848-8199** and ask for representative **#597**. The Starter Kit Includes:

■ Personal ID number and password

■ $15 credit on the system

■ Subscription to CompuServe Magazine

HERE'S HOW TO PLUG INTO PHCP:

Once on the CompuServe System, type any of these phrases to access the PHCP Forum:

GO PHCP	**GO BRADY**
GO QUEBOOKS	**GO HAYDEN**
GO SAMS	**GO QUESOFT**
GO NEWRIDERS	**GO PARAMOUNTINTER**
GO ALPHA	

Once you're on the CompuServe Information Service, be sure to take advantage of all of CompuServe's resources. CompuServe is home to more than 1,700 products and services—plus it has over 1.5 million members worldwide. You'll find valuable online reference materials, travel and investor services, electronic mail, weather updates, leisure-time games and hassle-free shopping (no jam-packed parking lots or crowded stores).

Seek out the hundreds of other forums that populate CompuServe. Covering diverse topics such as pet care, rock music, cooking, and political issues, you're sure to find others with the sames concerns as you—and expand your knowledge at the same time.